SQUAT

John Safran is a Melbourne writer and filmmaker. *Puff Piece* was shortlisted for the Prime Minister's Literary Awards, *Murder in Mississippi* won the Ned Kelly Award for Best True Crime. *John Safran's Music Jamboree* and *John Safran vs God* earned Australian Film Institute awards for Best Comedy Series and Outstanding Achievement in Craft in Television.

ALSO BY JOHN SAFRAN

Murder in Mississippi
Depends What You Mean by Extremist
Puff Piece

JOHN SAFRAN
SQUAT

PENGUIN BOOKS

UK | USA | Canada | Ireland | Australia
India | New Zealand | South Africa | China

Penguin Books is part of the Penguin Random House group of companies, whose addresses can be found at global.penguinrandomhouse.com.

First published by Penguin Books, 2024

Text copyright © John Safran, 2024

The moral right of the author has been asserted.

All rights reserved. No part of this publication may be reproduced, published, performed in public or communicated to the public in any form or by any means without prior written permission from Penguin Random House Australia Pty Ltd or its authorised licensees.

Cover design by Adam Laszczuk © Penguin Random House Australia Pty Ltd
Cover images courtesy Antoinette Barbouttis and Igor Madjinca/Stocksy
Typeset in Adobe Caslon Pro by Midland Typesetters, Australia

Printed and bound in Australia by Griffin Press, an accredited
ISO AS/NZS 14001 Environmental Management Systems printer

 A catalogue record for this book is available from the National Library of Australia

ISBN 978 1 76089 017 9

penguin.com.au

We at Penguin Random House Australia acknowledge that Aboriginal and Torres Strait Islander peoples are the Traditional Custodians and the first storytellers of the lands on which we live and work. We honour Aboriginal and Torres Strait Islander peoples' continuous connection to Country, waters, skies and communities. We celebrate Aboriginal and Torres Strait Islander stories, traditions and living cultures; and we pay our respects to Elders past and present.

For Seaweed

Antoinette Barbouttis contributed creative ideas and research that enlivened this book.

PROLOGUE

Seven months after I fled Kanye's mansion in Los Angeles, a rally for Palestine was held on the steps of the Sydney Opera House. This was in the days immediately after Hamas's attack on Israel, when Israel had just begun its military response. A video soon circulated purporting to show an ugly scene of protesters at the rally chanting nasty things about Jews. But some people were suspicious. The news outlet Crikey was concerned the video had been doctored, the protesters unfairly maligned. Some argued that because the subtitles on the video read 'Gas the Jews', we were being tricked into thinking that's what was being chanted, when in fact it was 'Where's the Jews?' Others thought these sceptics nuts, insisting they could most certainly hear the word 'gas'. As if a crowd shouting 'Where's the Jews?' wasn't ominous enough. 'Fuck the Jews' was also chanted, or wasn't, depending on who you asked.

So, what *was* chanted, and by how many? I was there that night, so I can tell you what I heard and saw.

PROLOGUE

Prior to the rally, NSW Police told Jewish Australians they should stay away from the Sydney Opera House.

So, I turned up to the Sydney Opera House.

By the time I got there, night had fallen. Maybe twenty minutes after we arrived, my girlfriend Antoinette and I were approached by a woman and half a dozen of her friends.

'You guys are Jews, aren't you?' the woman said.

'I'm Greek Orthodox,' Antoinette said.

I told her, yes, I was a Jew.

'You're undercover?' the woman continued.

From her question, I deduced she didn't know who I was (the nerve!); she didn't have a DVD of *John Safran's Music Jamboree* on her shelf. Rather, we struck her as suspicious because we were standing on our own, looking like we weren't a part of things. It became clear that a point of contention was that some rally-goers nearby were flinging flares at the police, and that I, observing this, might later claim to outsiders that all rally-goers were flinging flares. All rally-goers were not. Like most rallies, this was a stew of peace and chaos. There were people from all walks of life. Nearby, an Arab dad, not looking where he was going, was tripping over the candles laid on the ground to spell out 'Free Palestine'. A popular cry for peace is that Jews and Palestinians should stand together because they are so similar. Indeed, my clumsy dad, too, would have been tripping over those candles if he'd been there.

A friend of the woman talking to us interjected. 'Seventy-five years of occupying our lands. Where's justice?' she shouted. 'The Bible map, 1905, Israel never existed. Never existed!'

(I later learnt a video was doing the rounds online where an

American Christian showed a Bible from 1905 that featured a map marked 'Palestine', not 'Israel'.)

She continued, and, egged on by her passion, a crowd of men gathered around us, chanting 'Allahu Akbar! Allahu Akbar!'

I was taking this escalation better than Antoinette. She tried to calm things down by making a connection, bringing up the Greeks and the Islamic Ottoman Empire. She pleaded: were her people not the little guy of that conflict? Was history not tangled?

Ignoring her, a man pushed his phone in my face. The image on the screen was the Israeli flag, the Star of David replaced with a blue version of the poo emoji.

'Do your research, in the Bible, map 1905!' the woman repeated.

A man in a grey plastic mask stuck up his middle finger. 'She told you. Fuck you.'

I had thought I might be a 'good Jew'. Since my university days, anti-Israel protesters had told me that they have no beef with Jews per se, just the ones who had settled on the land marked Palestine on that Bible map. But here I was, 14,000 kilometres from there, and I was learning that the steps of the Sydney Opera House were another contested territory.

Observing the rising drama, two police officers swooped in, and I was frogmarched off. The protesters cheered the cops leading me away, their creed of All Cops Are Bastards temporarily parked to one side.

'Just go that way,' the cop told me. 'Just go that way. Just go that way. Behind the fence.'

'Why are you pushing me?' I complained. 'It's pretty messed up. I'm just standing there doing nothing and then they discovered

PROLOGUE

I was Jewish and then I had to go. And I did nothing except be Jewish.'

'Yeah, just in relation to ... we're just making sure you're safe.'

NSW Police had told Jewish people not to turn up here and these cops were following through. I was instructed to leave the precinct.

So, circling back to the original question. Was there antisemitism at the Sydney Opera House rally that night? And, if so, at what level?

I can't tell you, because I was thrown out for being a Jew.

SEVEN MONTHS EARLIER: BUMBLING

I've been in Los Angeles half a day. This is seven months before the war in Gaza. I'm in the bumbling stage of book writing, driving to dead ends while the half-thoughts, the no-thoughts and the overthinking are congealing.

I'm riding shotgun. Antoinette is cutting through the woods, squinting through the windscreen of the Jeep. Driving out of downtown Los Angeles, I'm surprised by how quickly things turn lush and mossy.

'I'm scared of being shot,' Antoinette says. I can't blame her. Yesterday I read a story about a man called Michael Dunn who fatally shot another man in a Texas car park. Wanting to know more, I googled, but I soon became confused by conflicting details in different news articles. Then it fell into place – a *different* Michael Dunn had also fatally shot somebody, this time at a gas station in Florida.

'Oh, there's a cat,' Antoinette sings out, forgetting about Americans and guns. She likes cats. She likes all creatures in the animal kingdom besides mosquitos and her family. I've only known Antoinette five months.

By the time I swoosh my head around, the cat has sprung away.

The dirt road opens to a clearing, revealing a small weatherboard house. A coop sits out front, occupied by a chicken that Antoinette also likes.

'It's not my book,' she says, meaning I should be the one to knock on this stranger's door.

'So, is this where it is *now*?' I ask, hopping out of the Jeep. 'Or it's not operational yet – it's opening at a later date?'

'Jesus! I don't know, John.'

There is so much contradictory information out there. This could be the place, or it couldn't.

I approach the house, unnerved that the loudest sound I can hear is my own footsteps.

That problem soon goes away, as my knock activates the psycho barking of a dog somewhere inside. A man, twenty-something, with a beard and no moustache, pokes his head out.

I say, 'I heard the Donda Academy might be starting up somewhere around here?'

Donda West, who passed away in 2007, was Kanye West's mother. He has named his secretive – and unaccredited – school after her.

'Yeah, it's right next door,' the man offers happily.

Following the man's finger, through the trees I can make out a fence covered by black tarpaulin. The length of the fence is hard to figure out from my vantage point.

'It's been vacant for months now,' he says. 'They were there for, like, a month, and after that it's just been vacant.'

I wander over to the fence, sizing it up, leaving Antoinette in the Jeep. I'm used to snooping solo and am still getting my head around this new arrangement. Antoinette is anxious about the danger in this unknown territory, so I've concluded that being left in the safety of a locked car is what she wants.

The chain-wire fence, one and a half times my height, runs all the way back to the main road, where we had turned off to enter the woods. Stretched tight as a drum, the black tarpaulin not only blocks lookie-loos, it prevents my fingers from finding any grip. I look about and consider climbing a tree and dropping over.

'I can probably go under there,' comes Antoinette's voice. 'I'm a rabbit.'

I turn around and see she's strolling over to me. Yes, I reckon she could squeeze under the fence, with a little burrowing and a shove from my foot. But sensing there is another way, we follow the boundary deeper into the woods, where we arrive at a section of fence that has collapsed.

(Crawling over the warped chain wire, it does not occur to me that a fence doesn't just collapse. Something, or someone, forces it down.)

The morning sunlight has cracked through the clouds. Once we're on the property, we see that down a slope, upon the richest and shiniest of grass, sits a schoolhouse painted entirely matte black.

Jack and Jill go down the hill. I find an unlocked window and begin boosting myself up. My approach is ungainly – a thread from my jumper catches on a screw, and my bottom is wiggling all about, but I manage to drop myself into the schoolhouse.

'The door's open,' Antoinette says, stepping through the nearby doorway.

Outside, sounds are gentle – the blowing of the wind, the chirping of birds, the rustling of leaves. Inside, sound is absent.

'Hello?' Antoinette tries. Her call is left unanswered.

Actually, maybe it isn't. Turning my head in this big grey room, I see the Almighty had something to say. Chalked in white in the middle of one wall: *And you shall love the LORD your God with all your heart and with all your soul and with all your mind and with all your strength.*

Because there are no furnishings, it's difficult to deduce the specific purpose of this room.

I disappear down a short staircase, into another large grey space. Dozens of envelopes are strewn across the concrete floor, coated in dust. Many are unopened utility bills addressed to the Donda Academy. Does this mean Kanye can't pay his bills, or just that he doesn't care to? Other envelopes are addressed to Kanye personally, the lettering jagged and blotchy. Crouching, flicking through them, I'm guessing these are fan mail. Whatever line I crossed jumping the fence, I won't cross another. I return the envelopes to the floor unopened.

Does this decision come down to Antoinette being here? It's too early in our relationship to have worked out her attitude to mail tampering. If I rip Kanye's mail open, maybe she'll think I'm a monster and catch the first flight back to Sydney. Or I'm just trying to assuage my guilt, like hardened criminals trying to convince themselves they're decent. 'Sure, I'd jump a person's fence, but I'd never open their mail' being my version of 'Yes, I've killed people, but I'd never kick a dog'.

A chill hits. Even in California, winter is running its course and the schoolhouse offers no relief. If anything, it's colder in here than outside.

'John?'

Antoinette finds me and leads me back up the short staircase, across the room with the Bible verse chalked on the wall, to a hallway. On either side, doors lead to smaller grey rooms. She ushers me into the first one, pointing to a notepad of enormous dimensions, maybe one square metre, resting on the floor.

'That's Kanye's handwriting for sure,' says Antoinette.

I knew she was a long-time fan, but not to the point that she could pick his penmanship.

Scribbled on this pad in black marker are 'Goals 4 the week', labelled 'Monday 9th – Saturday 14th January 2023'. That was two months ago.

The goals include 'sketch compound' and 'stretch daily'. 'Compound' is an ominous word. Respectable members of society stick with houses and apartments.

Also on this to-do list are 'email Alex Jones' and 'dog walker?'

I know Kanye has been a guest on *The Alex Jones Show*, with the podcast host considered by many to be a dangerous conspiracy theorist. So that task on the to-do list checks out. But whether Kanye wishes to employ a dog walker or is looking to get into the profession himself (maybe to pay those utility bills?) I do not know.

The window is lighting up dust particles floating through the air. I had thought that aside from the notepad the room was empty, but I now see that is untrue. A scroll of pinkish cardboard is propped up in the corner. Unrolling and pinning it to the ground, it turns out to be a map: a professionally drafted blueprint of the schoolhouse and surrounding area. A less graceful hand has made an addition: in thick felt-tip, with hectic up and down lines, someone has drawn a black rectangle. Is that the compound mentioned on the to-do list? If it is, it's going to be assembled next to this schoolhouse.

We wander up to the next room. Stacked on the floor there is children's artwork. Monsters, people, cars and planes, frenetically rendered in crayon and paint. Each piece is tagged with the name of the child artist. 'They're his kids.' Antoinette squats and retrieves paintings by Chicago and Psalm, the younger of the four children Kanye shares with his ex-wife, Kim Kardashian.

Antoinette is not impressed by the work of the toddlers. 'At their age, I was drawing people that looked like people.'

I guess she holds authority in the field of art criticism, having won Western Australia's Lester Prize for Portraiture in 2018. But she was thirty at the time. I'll need to view her folio from her kindergarten years before coming down too harshly on Chicago and Psalm.

'The one that's got serious talent is North West,' she adds.

Other rooms reveal brooms, a box of dinosaur books, more Bible quotes on the walls, and a bathroom with thick rings of scum around the bath and toilet bowl.

The end of the hallway opens up to another large room. Welcoming us, sparkling in the centre of the floor, is a bicycle. Laid out next to it, a cardboard sign: 'WHERE IS YE? FREE KANYE WEST! HELP FIND YE! SHARE ALL OVER SOCIAL MEDIA! YE! LET US KNOW YOU'RE OKAY!'

This sign corroborates what TMZ and other tabloid sites have been saying. Kanye is missing.

There's a phone number on the sign and I scribble it down. Then we decide to scoot, lest we push our luck.

Antoinette eases the Jeep out the woods, picking up speed as we hit the highway.

'I can't believe we did that. So fucking funny, John. Do you know my friends would die if they found out I've broken into . . .' she peters out, distracted by horses in the big green yards by the roadside. She snaps back to attention. 'My adrenaline is still going, because my mouth is very dry. Aren't you glad we hired a car? Strange place out here, reception for just one radio station. I am feeling pretty stressed. It's that naughty adrenaline, that I feel more guilty than good about, but, in hindsight, I'm actually fine about it. I was scared that someone was going to come in. I started knocking on the classroom doors when I couldn't find you, because for some reason you think a woman is safe in an abandoned building.'

I take note of what she expects when it comes to trespassing. It'll turn out this is more important than I realise at the time.

'Did you take a photo of me in the school?' she asks.

'Yep.'

'Good.'

THE SOUNDTRACK TO OUR ESCAPE

I hope I haven't been explaining this wrong. Since climbing over the collapsed fence, the adrenaline has been ricocheting through me, too. It's like the rush of a rollercoaster ride, one at an old amusement park, where you fear they haven't checked whether the bolts are still screwed tight enough. A policeman or a Kanye security guard might truly have come. With a gun.

But now that we've escaped the schoolhouse, charging down the highway, I can relish that feeling.

Antoinette puts on Kanye, bass pounding through the speakers of the Jeep.

In high school, hip-hop had me under a cult-like spell; LL Cool J blasting as I tackled homework, cassettes of the Beastie Boys and Run DMC strewn across the bedroom floor. I was possibly more into Public Enemy than the members of Public Enemy.

By the time Kanye dropped his first album in 2004, *College Dropout*, my palate had expanded. I still loved rap, but not quite so fervently. Hearing Kanye's music over the years, I thought it was pretty good, in the same way I thought the music of Slayer, Beethoven and other artists I wasn't emotionally invested in – and couldn't name too many tunes by – was pretty good.

For one straight hour in the Jeep, Antoinette and I don't talk. Instead of hearing Kanye's music in chunks and shreds, as background music at parties, I can really soak it in now. Him telling the story of blood-diamond mines, another track about monsters, another with a King Crimson sample.

This guy is brilliant. I wish I'd done this earlier – immersed myself in his tunes. If I had, I would have bounced over the collapsed fence with more pep in my step. I would have slid down the schoolhouse hallway like Tom Cruise in his underpants in *Risky Business*.

WHY AM I HERE, ANYWAY?

Seven months from now I'll turn up to the Sydney Opera House because I'm told, as a Jew, not to. I've come to LA on a similar impulse. Back in 2005, in his hit 'Gold Digger', Kanye complained that women were after his wallet. But by October 2022 he was airing his grievances about another group of alleged gold diggers. The Jews.

Having rechristened himself Ye, he posted on social media, 'I'm a bit sleepy tonight but when I wake up I'm going death con 3 On JEWISH PEOPLE'. A threat in the form of a pun, DEFCON being the alert system that prepares the US military for war.

By now also a fashion designer, Kanye had partnered with Adidas on his Yeezy range of sneakers. It was later revealed that, over his decade-long collaboration with Adidas, he had allegedly drawn a swastika on a sneaker in a meeting with them and told a Jewish executive to kiss a picture of Adolf Hitler. But that had been behind closed doors. Now he wanted to get things off his chest publicly.

He pushed the notion that Jews were cunning with money and greedier than non-Jews, tropes going back thousands of years.

He told Fox News host Tucker Carlson, 'I prefer my kids knew Hanukah than Kwanzaa – at least it will come with some financial engineering.'

I reached into my memory, thinking about my decades of Hanukkahs. When had I learnt about financial engineering? I guess there is a festive spinning-top game where, depending how the dreidel lands, you lose or gain a chocolate coin. But Anglicans put a coin in their Christmas pudding, with whoever gets the lucky slice being the winner, and Kanye hasn't turned that into a global plot.

Another trope he's pushed is that Jews lurk in the shadows, orchestrating events behind the scenes; when you hit an obstacle in life, it's the Jews holding you back. Showcasing his Yeezy collection at Paris Fashion Week, the same month as the Fox News interview, both he and his models sported 'White Lives Matter' t-shirts. Artists like Sean 'Diddy' Combs and John Legend rebuked him; presumably because they felt he was undermining or mocking the Black Lives Matter movement. Kanye, however, blamed their criticism on the Jews, posting online the message he sent Combs: 'Imma use you as an example to show the Jewish people that told you to call me that no one can threaten or influence me.'

Two months after that first social media post, in December 2022, Kanye pulled on a black balaclava with no eyeholes and took a seat on the set of *The Alex Jones Show*. His Bible resting before him, he began philosophising to millions, 'Every human being has brought something of value. Especially Hitler.'

In among all this, Adidas ended their partnership. Kanye's outbursts were a nightmare for them, conjuring ghosts from the past. You wouldn't know this from the 'company history' section on the Adidas website, which is expansive enough to include that Run DMC penned an ode to their sneakers in 1986 but leaves out that its founders, brothers Adolf and Rudolf Dassler, were members of the Nazi party, and that Adidas supplied shoes to the armed forces of the Third Reich.

Business magazine *Forbes* estimated that in losing this deal, Kanye's net worth tumbled from $2 billion to $400 million.

THEY NOT LIKE US

Kanye's situation – criticise Jews and get fired – led some people to suggest that, well, hadn't that proved his point?

Marque Lawyers is a progressive Sydney law firm. When Pauline Hanson tweeted that fellow senator Mehreen Faruqi should 'piss off back to Pakistan', they started court proceedings on her behalf, insisting that Hanson had breached the racial discrimination act.

But it was a tweet from Marque Lawyers that got *my* goat. When Adidas dumped Kanye, they wrote, 'It's interesting that anti-Semitic speech is the only form of racism that operates absolutely to exclude a person from polite society in the US. Not that it shouldn't do that, but surely all racist hate speech should have the same consequence.'

This was so frustrating! I immediately pulled up the Notes app on my phone and began bashing out a letter of complaint.

Dear Marque Lawyers,
Jewish American comedian Roseanne Barr was fired from her top-rating television show in 2018 for tweets comparing a Black politician to a monkey in Planet of the Apes. *For pushing anti-Muslim views, Jewish Republican candidate Laura Loomer was deplatformed from Facebook, Twitter, Instagram, Uber, Lyft, Uber Eats, PayPal, Venmo, GoFundMe, Periscope, Medium and TeeSpring. So I'd like to rise and shout 'Objection!' to your claim that: 'It's interesting that anti-Semitic speech is the only form of racism that operates absolutely to exclude a person from polite society in the US.' For better or worse, the last decade has been characterised by the nonstop deplatforming of people – including Jews! – who push the wrong buttons around race and religion, so I reckon your take on antisemitic speech being treated differently than other hate speech is baloney.*

I closed the Notes app on my phone, but not before observing this was my 732nd grievance against the world that I hadn't followed up on.

Marque Lawyers are the opposite of Kanye. They're progressive while he's an avowed Hitler enthusiast. Yet when it came to the Jews, they effortlessly – probably unintentionally – alluded to the idea that there's *something* about the Jews that makes them different from everyone else.

SLURS

Downtown Los Angeles has a brand-new funk. One I don't recall from the last time I visited, a decade ago. It's the smell of weed. Back then, you had to stand in a room of weed smokers to catch the aroma. Now it hits you, again and again, as you shuffle down the street. I haven't a clue why the fragrance hangs about, long after those who vape have disappeared, rather than dissolving into the endless California sky. Most oddly, the smell finds its way into your car, through the vents, even as you rush down the highway.

We made our getaway from the schoolhouse an hour ago. Antoinette has pulled over and we're sipping juices on a bench outside a department store, taking in the vista of a strip-mall car park.

'So, Kanye is not paying his bills.'

I'm thinking about the envelopes, coated in dust, on the floor of the schoolhouse.

'He's very focused on how much he's been ripped off, and he's not paying his own bills,' Antoinette says.

She's right, it is interesting – even without the Adidas partnership, isn't Kanye loaded? I have no clue what to make of it.

There was one item in the schoolhouse that was *not* coated in dust.

'Why would there be such a fresh bike there?' I ask.

'I think someone is squatting there.' She rests her juice on the bench. 'Do you reckon it could be Kanye?'

There's one way to find out.

Might as well keep going. That's how the bumbling works.

I unfold the sheet of paper on which I had scribbled down the phone number from the cardboard sign we'd found next to the bicycle. I tap the digits out on my phone; eventually someone picks up.

'G'day?' I begin.

'Who is this?' It's a man, and he's a mumbler.

I tell him who I am and how I got his number. He's confused. He squeezes out a 'Whaaaat?'

We go in circles until his ears acclimatise to my accent. He says he didn't write the sign, but he knows who did and he'll find out if that person wants to talk to me. He hangs up.

'Did it sound like Kanye?' Antoinette asks.

'Well, he wasn't autotuned or anything.'

'Kanye hasn't been T-Pain autotuned for a long time,' Antoinette says, fact-checking my joke.

The red button glowing on my audio recorder, resting in my lap, catches her eye.

'Don't ever play my voice back to me, because I'll have a nervous breakdown. It's like showing me photos of myself with bad skin.'

She does want to have her say, though. She picks up the recorder.

'It's an absolute privilege – for John – to have me break into the former Donda Academy with him. Because as a fan that's followed him for thirteen years, you get to know Kanye's handwriting and that he only writes with a black texta in capitals. So I'm able to then be like: this is definitely Kanye. And that's why – and John might think the contrary – but I'm closer to thinking that the man on the phone could be Kanye West. Maybe he went out to spread his own myth about being missing.'

My phone buzzes again; the number coming up on the screen is the same one I just called.

Antoinette grabs the phone from me.

'Who are you?' she asks. 'What's your name?'

'My name is James,' slurs this man.

'Were you the person who wrote the sign trying to find Kanye?'

'That person ain't here. Shoot, I'm sorry.'

She looks at me and shakes her head to convey that this isn't Kanye's voice. It's also not the voice of the man who was on the phone before. James begins discussing SIM cards, how his was switched with another person's. His voice slurs more and more, until he sounds like bubbling porridge.

But Antoinette is not finished with the matter of Kanye. Her intuition grips on to something else.

'Are you with Kanye right now?' she asks.

After a long silence he manages an 'um'. She interprets this as him being evasive.

'Are you with Kanye at present?' she insists.

'I've got to go.' He sounds frightened.

'You *are* with Kanye.'

'I'm not with Kanye, okay.' Something she has said has piqued his interest, though. He asks, 'What do you want to give him for a present?'

Antoinette is confused. 'What do I want to give him as a present?'

I immediately spot the source of the confusion. A homonym is a word holding more than one meaning. The two people in this conversation have chosen 'present' to mean two different things.

Regardless, this promise of a gift pulls James out of his slurring.

'What do you want to give him? I'll have him call you right now.'

'Okay, get him to call me. That'd be great.'

'Yeah, if you Cash App me first.'

We learn this is a mobile payment service.

Antoinette and James agree on fifty bucks. He spells out his account name – 'M as in Michael. U as in umbrella. S as in shit . . .'

We soon discover Australian phones don't allow this Cash App.

I shout-whisper that we should meet him face to face, promising to give him the fifty bucks in person.

'We're in Orange County right now,' James says. 'We've just had to come to check out a new studio here.'

I'm trying to keep up. So Kanye is with him right now? And they're looking over a recording studio?

'Where's the studio?' Antoinette asks.

'Newport Beach. I don't know what the studio name is. I got to ask him, but I can't now. He's inside there right now talking to the – I guess the head honcho.'

Antoinette arranges a meet-up at a diner in Orange County,

an hour's drive from downtown Los Angeles. James says he'll be bringing his business partner.

They hang up and I say, 'You reckon Kanye's with him?'

'Absolutely not, John.' She laughs. 'I'll drive you, but I'm not getting out. You can talk to this loony. I'm scared as hell.'

On the drive to Orange County, Antoinette is unusually quiet. When she finally has something to say, it's this: 'The more I think about it, the more I'm thinking this is part of Kanye's world. It could be Kanye gone way off the rails.'

DREAM CHASER

We squeak across a vinyl-upholstered booth in the diner. Light fittings that look like fifties B-52 hairdos hang from the orange ceiling. Antoinette did end up getting out of the Jeep.

'I looked like Mischa Barton,' Antoinette is telling me for the third time, referring to an actor from *The O.C.*, an early-2000s teen drama set here. She's prosecuting her case, pulling up headshots of the star, when two young men wander over, grasping backpacks and plastic bags full of clothes. They slide into the other side of the booth.

James, only hours ago a disembodied voice, now sits before me, flesh and blood. He is a handsome man, Hispanic and German roots, with a pencil moustache and cheekbones that could take out an eye.

That turn of phrase must have popped into my head because the fellow he has brought along, his business partner, is missing one eye. The socket looks like pursed lips. Two mouths, one face. His name is Kai. Notably absent from this meeting – Kanye West.

I tell them lunch is on me; pancakes, biscuits and gravy, coffee.

'I didn't know who you were. But I looked you up.' James points a spoon my way. 'I'm aware of what you're doing. And you're a dream chaser, correct?'

'Yes. Dream chaser. That's it. Why not?'

Over the phone, James had insisted he hadn't made the cardboard sign at the schoolhouse. He now reveals that he did. And the bike is his too.

'I've been in juvenile detention seventeen times. I have over thirty arrests in the state of Connecticut,' he says. 'I've been on drugs, I've been homeless. I have made good money. I have worn suits and ties.'

Today he wears a crisp white t-shirt and grey camouflage pants. However, a few months back he was working in sales in Connecticut. Then one day everything changed.

'God told me to get up and go find Kanye. So I got up and I went to find Kanye. That same day, I quit my job. I packed my bags. I got on a train. You don't even know what fucking pain I went through to make that happen.'

It took a bus, two trains and four hours on foot to arrive at the woods in Simi Valley. Like we had, James reached the chain-wire fence, blacked out with tarpaulin. He was the one who had forced down the fence that Antoinette and I crawled over. Like we had, he looked down the hill, intrigued by the sight of a matte black schoolhouse in the rich green grass. It matched visions he'd had.

'I built that school in my head before it was there. You understand? I wanted to work there. I went to go find Kanye.'

Like we had, he found the schoolhouse Kanyeless.

'Unfortunately, I don't know if I'll ever meet Kanye. But that's okay. I barely want to listen to anybody else's music, because I just love him. And he's me. I believe in reincarnation. Reincarnation is true. When I see him talk, it's like me. My family – my mom, she sees me in him. We're born two days apart. We're Geminis. In the same decan. Whatever the fuck that means. I don't even know. Astrologers split it up into, like, six days. We're in the same week.'

Having quit his job and lost his income, he needed somewhere to lodge, so he moved into the schoolhouse. He has since vacated the property.

'How many nights did you stay there?' I ask.

James rises, commanding the booth, drawing us in with the captivating cadence of a preacher in the pulpit. 'Twenty-five nights, twenty-six days.'

'Wow. And no one turned up?'

He says that a bald, heavy-set white man, who worked for Kanye, came by and kicked him out on the twenty-sixth day. 'There were two others with this man, in Donda Academy shirts. One was very, very nervous. Like he knew he was doing something wrong by throwing me out.'

James returns to his seat. He says the Bible quotes chalked on the walls were already there when he arrived and are by Kanye's hand. However, the to-do list on the giant notepad was not Kanye's – James was the one who penned the list about contacting Alex Jones and a dog walker. This debunks Antoinette's claim that she can recognise Kanye's handwriting, but I leave that unsaid, because I am not a petty man.

Antoinette remembers one of the tasks on the to-do list. 'You had on it: "sketch the compound". So are you an artist, then?'

'Hell no,' James says. 'I've been dreaming of building off-grid communities, I've —'

Antoinette butts in. 'So it's not for art's sake that you want to sketch the compound?'

James ignores her question. 'I've already seen it in my head a thousand times.'

But Antoinette won't let go of the notion that this could be art.

'What if you just started sketching it and then make that into art and then that's something you can —'

'It's not art!' James snaps.

A few months earlier, Antoinette pulled a book from her shelf, *Who's Afraid of Conceptual Art?*, and encouraged me to read it. I seem to recall, according to the book, that *intention* is a prerequisite for something to be considered art.

The waitress is refilling James's coffee as he moves on to pushing the case for Jesus. He says I shouldn't discount His truth just because I was brought up Jewish.

'There's truth and lies in everything,' he preaches.

This prompts his business partner to put down his fork.

'And I wanted to open my mouth too,' Kai says. 'Because I know that — and this is an assumption that I do not have the right to make — but I know that with you guys sitting on that side of the table, looking at me, I probably look Mexican. I probably look like a gang member. I probably look like my eye got shot. Yeah. And that's fine. I'm not mad if you guys are seeing it that way. But what I'm saying is — the reason why I wanted to open my mouth is because I'm so much more than that. I'm actually not Mexican. I'm from Hawaii. I lost my eye to a tumour. Thank God, they got it out.'

His story fills my mind with all kinds of vivid images – gangs, bullets, Hawaii, surgeons stitching skin. Just as Antoinette thinks James should be an artist, I'm thinking Kai should write.

'I was wondering when I was going to find out,' James says. 'I'm just learning this stuff.'

It's odd that Kai's missing eye hadn't come up before. I ask how long they've been friends.

'It's like we've been soul brothers that have been lost on earth forever,' James says.

'We're twins,' adds Kai.

'But how long have you known each other?'

'I met him this morning,' James says.

He explains that they're staying at a nearby hotel that 'isn't the Ritz'.

Then he locks his eyes on Antoinette. 'Do you love Kanye?'

'I love Kanye,' she says, like a schoolgirl cutting out photos of Duran Duran to stick on her exercise book. From the corner of my eye, I catch her quick guilty glance my way. This is a tricky question for her, what with her boyfriend being a Jew.

James senses something's up. 'What's burdening you?'

'I was a big Kanye fan,' she says. 'I think he went a bit too far.'

'Why do you think he went too far?' He pouts, going through the formality of pretending he doesn't know exactly what she's talking about.

'I think spreading any kind of racism or any kind of hate or —'

'He didn't.'

'It can be interpreted that way. And that's the problem. People will interpret it that way. Whether you like it or not. That's how people are. And they did. And I'm not Jewish. I grew up Christian.'

'Whose problem is that?'

'It can become a problem for the Jewish community in my area in Sydney. And they happen to be my friends.'

Go Antoinette!

'Why? How can it cause a problem for them? That he just says that he loves everybody?'

'That's not the problem.'

'Because he says he loves Hitler?'

Yes, James. Over the years I've learnt that people push hate through subtext. So if you say you love everything, it makes a difference whether you choose as your example butterflies or the tumour that ate Kai's eye.

'Who do you think promotes what you're speaking of?' James narrows his eyes. 'The misinterpretation. Because that's promoted. They specifically quoted "I love Hitler" out of a two-hour interview on *Alex Jones*, you see? So that was done. And who owns the media?'

Sometimes 'everyday' Jews hear some unbelievable things from people who don't realise they're Jewish, but because of my line of work, I'm privy to a lot of conversations like these.

It's not new to me. As a teenager, I would visit an esoteric bookstore in Melbourne. One shelf began with books on aliens. Running my finger along the spines, it eased into books on the government cover-up of the JFK assassination. Then came encyclopedias on secret societies. By the time my finger reached the end of the shelf, it was brushing books expounding the theory that Jews control the world.

So James's sudden diversion into 'The Jews' isn't an unexpected plot twist, it's part of a tradition. The marble rolling down the wooden maze always ends up here. And what Kanye did, at the very least, was reassure James that he was right to fear the Jews.

James shifts his attention to me.

'You thought you were coming here for Kanye. You don't realise that God called you here today. Jesus called you here today. You came here to find a relationship with Jesus Christ. You came here for freedom, from the constriction of your stupid Jewish religion.'

The writer in me can't believe his luck. What a quote! You can't make this stuff up. But when I turn to Antoinette, I see she has had a different reaction. She is flummoxed and upset. She asks the waitress for the cheque. Maybe I should think of the 99.99 per cent of Jews for whom slagging off the 'stupid Jewish religion' holds no creative benefits.

Before I can formulate a response to his various libels, James has moved on. Now he's clarifying his earlier thoughts on reincarnation. He believes that Kanye was killed, and that his ghost left his body and flew into James's. The Kanye now being snapped by paparazzi is a replica. The men who threw James out of the schoolhouse are in on this.

'This is a dangerous game,' James warns me. 'You're on a dangerous journey right now. So, obviously, either you're oblivious or you have some sort of cost–benefit analysis.'

'Yeah. It's probably the second one,' I say. 'The creative side of me is like: when you're feeling there's danger in where you're going, that's where the story is.'

SECOND HIT

The next morning, through the window of the ground-floor café in our hotel, I watch a dishevelled man crouch and empty his bowels onto the street. The hotel doorman's nonchalance as he speaks into his walkie-talkie suggests this is not a once-in-a-blue-moon event.

Antoinette has a lead on another Kanye haunt, one of the four properties Kanye owns in California (there might be more, depending on who you trust). Although she warns me this could turn out to be a red herring.

I offer to drive, but Antoinette says no. Pulling out from the hotel, she warns me never to leave her alone again. Now I've done it twice: at the schoolhouse and at the diner, where I nipped to the petrol station across the road to buy batteries for the audio recorder. Left alone with James and Kai, James started hitting on Antoinette. She asks me why I didn't learn from the schoolhouse, and I don't have an answer.

On the freeway, out the window in the distance, the Hollywood sign evokes glamour for us tourists. I've never considered the actual hills upon which the enormous letters are bolted.

They began forming tens of millions of years ago, I read on my phone, the oldest rocks dating back two billion years. So, dinosaur fossils, not just celebrity handprints on the Hollywood Walk of Fame, are embedded into the earth here. Foreshadowing the archetypal Californian, they were herbivores.

I've really got to get over my surprise that a finger's click out of downtown LA, you begin falling into nature. Forty-five minutes north-west of our hotel, still in Los Angeles County, we reach the city of Calabasas, tucked into the foothills of the Santa Monica and Santa Susana mountains. Everything that's not the sky is green or brown. I spend so much of my life in the city, I've forgotten that a big open sky makes me feel like an ant.

We turn onto a road so absent of bustle, the squeak of a fence is the big event. When we pass a stable, even the horses are keeping quiet. Antoinette spots an owl in a tree, which I can't make out no matter how hard I look. I can't tell if there are people anywhere.

The Jeep creeps further down the road. Ranch-style homes sit on vast plots of land. To our left, that land reaches back, meeting the hills; to our right, with a squint, I can see it runs into the woods.

No doubt secrets hide behind the walls of these ranches, but the land itself is an open book – or at least appears to be. The sun pings a spotlight on each tractor, dirt bike, tin drum and rusted rake propped up on a porch. That's until we reach a property to our right. Is this Kanye's place?

Blocking the view is an epic metal gate, wide and tall, curved across the top. Matte black. A fence, also black, taller than me, stretches out either side.

We pull over and I slide out of the Jeep. There's a keypad on the gate, with numbers and letters, but no doorbell. The open sky that renders objects tiny can't work its magic here – the mansion behind the gate is just too damn big. Still, I can only make out portions, catching a little over the top of the gate. I try walking further back to see more, but I hit the front yard of the house on the other side of the road, so my view into the mansion remains blocked.

When I return with my findings, Antoinette is examining a photo she has saved from a real-estate website. She's in two minds about whether this is Kanye's place.

'I think that is – maybe? – it. It looks so different, though.'

She says builders could have renovated the place since the photo for the real-estate listing was taken, which would explain the discrepancy between what she sees in real life and what she sees on her phone.

'So, what's your latest thought?' I try.

'I can't get reception, so my latest thought is I don't have reception. From what I can see from a very blurred photo, it might be it. But I don't know.'

Antoinette hops out of the Jeep too, and together we stroll to the next plot of land, one down from the mansion. We're once again faced with a fence, but we can see through this one. And what we see is a muddy bank sharply descending to a stream, which is gushing furiously. If you jumped off the lip of the bank, it would be quite the fall before you hit the water. On the other side of the stream, another steep bank ascends to a thick mess of woods.

I'm trying to get my bearings. Do these woods belong to whoever owns the suspected Kanye mansion – is it attached to that property? Or is it a separate section of land, maybe a national park? I realise this stream must run through the property upon which the mansion sits, so, at the very least, it's connected that way.

We walk on, for quite a while, eyeing the woods on the other side of the stream. Then the fence just ends, and wild bushes begin. These serve the same function as the fence, blocking outsiders from wandering in. However, there is a design flaw. After the fence stops, but before the bushes start, there's a narrow gap you could slide through.

But it's no help for snoopers like me. Squeezing through here, you're just faced with the steep bank leading down to an uninviting stream.

With no easy way of going any further, we head back to the Jeep. In a reverse-psychology move, we parked close to the gate of the mansion. From the ranches across the road, neighbours could be peeking from any number of windows, but they'd think, those two must be on the straight and narrow, otherwise they wouldn't be making their presence so obvious.

Still, I'm feeling vulnerable. I've been meandering out the front of the mansion for too long, trying to work out what to do next. Something catches my eye. No wonder I didn't catch it before – it's at the level of my shoe. Forced into the gap between the gate and one of the pillars is an envelope. I squat down. The envelope is weathered and shows the logo of a water company.

It's addressed to Kanye West.

ERNIE THE NEIGHBOUR

At the place across the road from Kanye's mansion, a cross is planted in the front lawn as big as the one Jesus found himself on. Anywhere else, I'd assume this denotes a church. But this is America.

Inside, sitting on a couch not a pew, I start chatting with Ernie, a white gentleman in his seventies, who is the homeowner, not a cleric. Most items in Ernie's lounge room are brown, from the mantelpiece to his pants. The yellow glow from table lamps makes up for the heavy curtains blocking out the morning light.

Antoinette, fearing what was behind this door, is waiting in the Jeep. It seems there are exceptions to her rule of not being left alone. But then, she wants me to come and get her if it turns out everything is okay. I'm sipping the soup so she can determine if it's poisoned.

'So what's it like being a neighbour of his?' I ask Ernie. 'Is it fun?'

'No, it's terrible.'

Ernie settles back into his brown leather chair. 'When he first bought the property, we didn't think much of it. Or care. Then he started the domes – the homeless domes. They were like four storeys tall, great big things. And they were supposed to be prototypes for housing the homeless.'

Kanye began constructing these domes in 2019. The *Star Wars* toy homesteads he played with as a kid influenced the design of these gold and brown metallic beehives.

'He was going to bring in investors to buy these things for different parts of the area. And so that was all illegal. No permits, no nothing.'

They were known as his Yecosystem. I appreciate the pun; Ernie appreciates nothing about them.

'They were all up on the back of the property. We had some of our neighbours that were horse people that rode up in there and took some pictures.' He points through his wall to his yard. 'And I went way up on my hill there and tried to peek down.'

The horsemen called the city council.

'One of the problems was they were doing a lot of welding in a fire zone. We were afraid of brush fires.'

So Kanye is either the goodie for endeavouring to build shelter for the homeless or the baddie for presuming he didn't have to follow the law. And his neighbours are either heroes for taking steps to prevent bushfires, which have torn through this area before, or villains because that was a convenient cover for the real issue: the possibility of homeless people moving in. After all, Calabasas is one of the wealthiest cities in America.

'Finally, after five of 'em was complete, they made 'em tear 'em all down. So that came to an end.'

Now something unexpected and fun happens. Chimes begin

to bong – BONG, BONG, BONG – from a grandfather clock behind Ernie. A hefty black marble clock, resting among figurines on a cabinet, begins harmonising. These two clocks are so loud and resonant, for all I know they're drowning out other clocks elsewhere in the house. It's ten o'clock on a Saturday morning.

To top it all off, the doorbell starts bing-bonging.

'Shucks, just a second,' Ernie says.

It turns out Antoinette has decided to join us. Unlike me, she asks Ernie if she should remove her shoes. He says yes, leaving me looking ill-mannered, yet he motions 'don't bother' when I go to untie my shoes. We catch her up on the *Star Wars* beehives.

'Then he starts with his Yeezy church business,' Ernie continues.

Kanye built a church behind the mansion. I realise this must be an enormous plot of land.

'Again, at first we didn't think anything bad about it. But the hundreds and hundreds of people – there was so much traffic out on our street, we couldn't get out to go to church ourselves! Then the police started coming and patrolling it, and they said all the cars had to be off the pavement or they could ticket 'em.'

Ernie tolerates the grandfather clock, but even he has his limits.

'The music was kinda okay on Sunday morning, but the problem was during the week, when they practised loud. It would actually rattle our windows.'

There was more to come.

'Then he erected these huge, big metal columns, which made up a frame, and covered the whole mansion in white plastic.'

'What was the function of that?' I ask.

'Just to hide everything. Just to keep everything in a bubble.'

Then, one day, just like that, no more Sunday service, no more weekday rehearsals. But Kanye wasn't done.

'The next thing he did is brought in his day care. It was for little kids. It was called Yeezy Christian Academy. The kids wore garbs, and we didn't really care. That was all Christian and they weren't noisy.'

Ernie mightn't have minded, but the authorities shut it down. Kanye was running a business in a non-business zone, and one involving kids at that. But Yeezy Christian Academy evolved into Donda Academy, and moved to Simi Valley, where James had squatted and we had climbed the fallen fence ourselves.

'He was supposed to take the structure down. He never did.' He means the scaffolding and white plastic that kept the mansion across the road in a bubble. Ernie sometimes climbs his hill and looks down into Kanye's property. 'Finally, the sun and the wind destroyed the bubble. So it's basically all blown away now. So that's where he left it. He has never returned. And it sits.'

Ernie says the mansion has lain dormant for over a year. With only one spark of life.

'For the past year, he's had a guard there parked on the property twenty-four seven. We could hear the switching guards. The big gate opens, the big gate shuts. One leaving, one coming.'

I gulp at the implications of this. So a guard was watching me when I was stickybeaking at the gate? No doubt a guard can look out even though strangers can't look in.

But Ernie calms my nerves. 'That finally stopped, oh, a few weeks ago.'

One night the guard drove off and no one else substituted in.

'ERNIE THE NEIGHBOUR

Now, Ernie says, the only living creatures behind the gate would be those critters in the woods beyond the mansion. I draw my eyes to Antoinette and find she's also turned to look at me. We both know. This is promising.

GREGG THE OTHER NEIGHBOUR

Wandering up the road, the same side as the mansion, a white guy in his thirties is stacking boxes on his porch.

'My wife and kids and I really enjoyed it,' Gregg says of Kanye's Sunday service and the weekday rehearsals. Kanye's people had gone door to door, inviting neighbours to the service and a meal afterwards. He took up the offer, which Ernie had declined. 'They had a forty-person gospel choir, but Kanye was orchestrating the whole thing. And it was the gospel choir mixed in with modern R'n'B songs. It was really, really nice. And I thought it was all really positive for the neighbourhood. But I guess not everybody agreed.'

Ernie furnished us with good news: no guards. But Gregg delivers news that complicates matters for those aiming to sneak around this street. He points up a hill, across from his home.

'One neighbour, you can see, he has an observation deck up there.'

He's right – I can just make it out. From all the way down here, it's a tiny wooden box. The place is a few houses up from Ernie's. So another neighbour with a hill can look down into the goings-on behind Kanye's gate.

'I know that when Kanye was building those big domes, that neighbour in particular didn't care for it. A lot of those pictures that found their way into TMZ were taken from there.'

Paparazzi weren't doing stake-outs in the box; the neighbour snapped the shots himself. Was it to make money?

'No, no. I think it was another way of complaining. They are very affluent. They weren't out to get a few bucks from TMZ.' Gregg looks across the houses on the other side of the road. 'I don't know of anybody around here to be that way, but I certainly hope it wasn't at all racially motivated. But who knows?'

So, Kanye and I have at least one connection. No matter what we do, for people who don't like Black people he'll just be Black, and for people who don't like Jewish people I'll just be a Jew.

You don't have to assemble domes to raise ire around here. 'We have neighbours who love to complain. I have a tractor that, if I turn it on and drive it fifty feet on Sunday, or a holiday even – sometimes holidays I didn't even know existed – or before 7 am, or after 7 pm – then the sheriff immediately pulls in my driveway.'

So, this street is peppered with snitches. Ones happy to call in the cops. We hop back in the Jeep and decide not to press our luck. Kanye's mansion disappears behind us.

HATCHING THE PLAN

I'm about to make a life-changing decision.

I'm lost in a cable-knit jumper and a coat with a pulled-up hood, on a patio in Malibu, a seafood restaurant stopover between Calabasas and our hotel. The view would be gorgeous, but the clouds are being scumbags, blocking the sun from lighting up the sand and sea. We would have chosen an inside table if one had been available.

'You know when Nine Inch Nails wrote *The Downward Spiral*, they wrote and recorded it in the Charles Manson house?'

Antoinette is talking with her Greek hands more than usual. While Roman Polanski was in Europe, Manson's hench-kids broke in and killed his wife Sharon Tate, and five of her guests, and wrote 'Pig' on the front door in her blood. Two decades later, Trent Reznor and his musician pals took up residency at that Beverly Hills house.

'Maybe you need to write your book in the Donda Academy schoolhouse. Where James squatted. Try and write the book there the same way. It might be so dark and weird. That album did really well.'

It's not just this patio that's freezing – I remember the icy chill blowing through the schoolhouse yesterday, too.

'I like everything about it, but it's quite cold.'

'Nine Inch Nails did it.'

Yes, but what was the reading on the thermostat in the Charles Manson house when Trent Reznor pulled the microphone to his lips and belted out that he wanted to fuck his love interest like an animal?

I put down the calamari ring I'm halfway into and defend myself. 'I'm not trying to be soft.'

'It's coming to summer.'

It's coming to summer in three months! That said, I am coming around to the idea.

'I'll be in a hotel. I'm not staying there. But you should,' she says. 'Bring a lot of antihistamines. A lot of dust around there. Maybe get a duster as well.'

Apparently if I stay in the schoolhouse, I'll be both freezing and wheezing.

I look out to the sad beach. This prompts a thought of my own: why bunk-up at a dumpy schoolhouse when you can holiday at an LA celebrity mansion?

'Is the Calabasas mansion a bit of a nicer place to stay?'

Antoinette is thrown by this escalation. She rests her hands.

'I'm just worried that there are too many nosey neighbours. It's a multimillion-dollar place. People are more likely to go check on the mansion than the schoolhouse.'

She's staring at her salad, mulling something over. Then her eyes light up.

'You have to go into the mansion,' she says. 'Imagine if Kanye takes this Nazi stuff further. Imagine, say, that Kanye builds an army and, whatever, those crazy Christians follow him. Imagine if you could go back in time and get inside Hitler's house before he went ... before he went *Hitler*. There'd be a lot of stuff you could find. Imagine infiltrating a dictator's house. That's why you need to go in. To get Kanye's secrets. Yeah. Imagine getting the Gestapo's secrets before they became the Gestapo.'

My eyes have lit up too. This idea ticks a lot of boxes – pretty much every one – when it comes to my personal interests: Nazis, hip-hop, book writing and snooping.

This takes us to the matter of getting into the property. I know how to breach the schoolhouse fence, but how would I get onto the grounds of the mansion?

Ernie, the guy with the grandfather clock, said neighbours – horse people! – rode onto Kanye's property to snap photos. So they got in somehow. I don't reckon they trotted in through the front gate. I'm guessing the horse people entered Kanye's property from *behind*, through the woods at the back of the property.

Antoinette laughs. 'There's no better time to do it than right now. Now the guards are off. If a new guard comes, you're screwed.'

This is true. Yet the matter of the guards is not the only consideration – as part of my initial bumbling, I've set other plates spinning. I have other leads to chase. So I can't breach the walls of the mansion just yet.

'Wipe your face,' Antoinette says.

HATCHING THE PLAN

I wipe tartare sauce from my face, pull my diary from my bag, and pencil in the date that I hope to start my writer's residency at Kanye's mansion: one week from today.

I BLAME THE PARENTS

Lying in the hotel bed, digesting the calamari rings from a few hours ago, about to enter the land of nod, I imagine my father is in this room, measuring its dimensions. It's a fuzzy half-dream version of a memory.

When I was little, he would walk the perimeter of rooms, his stride serving as a tape measure. He was an internal auditor, which is a type of accountant, but he had always wanted to be an architect, and this explained his habit of needing to know the dimensions of rooms.

Now I'm picturing my father and me in tracksuits. I'm in primary school. We're jogging one morning when he stops outside a newly built house. He tells me he's fairly sure that no one has moved in yet. Then he leads me down the side of the house, squats, and boosts me up to the laundry window. My heart is racing as I squeeze through. I know this is wrong.

My feet find the washing machine and I secure my footing, then clamber down to the laundry floor. I creep through the house, the smell of cut wood competing with fresh paint. When I come to the front door I squeak it open, allowing my father in.

I make my way up the stairs and explore the place. I wander in and out of rooms, sticking my nose in closets and drawers. Looking down from the top of the stairs, I see my father in the front room: striding the perimeter, counting the metres, working out the dimensions.

We leave the house, adrenaline pounding through me, and jog away up the street. What a topsy-turvy morning for my little heart and brain – more intense than anything I have felt thus far in my short life. My first experience of the thrill of trespassing.

ONE WEEK LATER

We rush into a camping store and scramble shelf to shelf.

'I'm not good when things are last-minute and there's a lot to organise. I'm not good at that,' Antoinette says.

We sweep supplies into a large duffle bag:

Thirty-five-mile, twenty-two-channel, two-way walkie-talkies. We need these because we know our phones don't pick up reception in this part of Calabasas.

Sleeping bag.

Bear horn. Antoinette paid more attention than I did during our visit to the local nature museum yesterday. It wouldn't have occurred to me to pack one of these, even though California flaps it in your face: there's a bear on the state flag. Alongside black bears, mountain lions and coyotes also lurk in these woods. (I pull down my cap, embroidered with a mountain lion, as far over my ears as it will go.)

Bear repellent. Now that I think about it, it wouldn't have occurred to me to buy walkie-talkies either. Thank you, Antoinette!

ONE WEEK LATER

Two one-and-a-half-gallon jugs of water. If Kanye doesn't pay his utility bills, the water might be cut off. And a hand-held shovel. If the water's cut off, the toilets won't work, and I'll need that to dig holes.

The electricity could be cut off too, so a handheld lantern, a headlamp and a Dolphin torch.

Plenty of batteries.

First-aid kit, insect repellent, all-in-one screwdriver/wrench/nail puller, chewable electrolyte tablets, body wipes, toilet paper, *Pocket Guide to Animal Tracks*, *Wild Animals of California*, *Field Guide to Birds of California*, *California Plants: A guide to our iconic flora*, and a spork.

After the camping store, we hightail it to a supermarket, filling a second duffle bag with non-perishable food: powdered milk, canned vegetables, canned fruits, canned tuna, granola bars, beef jerky, chocolate, crackers, nachos, popcorn, peanut butter, honey and a box of after-dinner mints. I grab a bag of mandarins and bunch of bananas on the way to the register.

A day ago we moved from our hotel in downtown LA to one in Calabasas, and that's where we dash after the supermarket, squeezing clothes into the duffle bags. With all the other stuff already in there, space is tight.

'Do you reckon I just wear the same clothes? Like, "fuck changing my clothes"?'

Antoinette is chucking me toiletries from the hotel bathroom. 'Well, change your underwear so you don't get worms or something. What was the last thing you did like this?'

'I guess the last danger was hanging out with neo-Nazis.'

'Different kind of danger, though. Hanging out with neo-Nazis is less funny.' Then she remembered what Kanye said. 'This is a different version of hanging out with neo-Nazis, I suppose.'

I zip up the two duffle bags.

'You've still got to put pants on.'

And with those immortal words, we rush to the hotel car park and fang it.

THE MOMENT ARRIVES

The Jeep creeps down a familiar street in Calabasas, pulling closer and closer to Kanye's mansion.

Over the last week, I've learnt more about my new quarters. The mansion was initially the dedicated headquarters for his Sunday Service church. But after he split with Kim in early 2021, he turned it into a bachelor pad, living there with Russian model Irina Shayk.

The grandfather clock, in the house across from the mansion, would be striking seven right now – seven in the evening.

I'm now thinking it is tactically wrong to have come at dusk; if we were wandering around during the daytime, we'd look less suspicious.

'Check that no guards have come back, obviously,' Antoinette says. 'Are you scared?'

'I'm not really scared yet. But I could be naive.'

'I think you're naive. But I think that's a good thing.'

'What are your feelings?' I ask.

'Oh my God. Can you not read them all over me? Am I not petrified? I'm so nervous and I don't want to leave you and be responsible for something happening to you because I'm dropping you off. So can you clear me of all of that?'

Is she scared I'll die? Or is she scared she'll cop the blame if I die?

'Sure,' I say. I have more immediate concerns. Will this even work? What if I can't get in? Or some neighbour spots me, derailing the adventure before it even begins? (Later I'll realise I should have been asking other questions. Is this a *crime* crime? Is this the type of antic where the local police call the consulate?)

We pull up outside the mansion. I reach over to the back seat for the duffle bag filled with food and slip out of the Jeep. Immediately, drizzle lands in tiny grey dots on my turquoise anorak. The rain feels rejuvenating on my face, my hands.

I make my way to the gate, get some momentum going in my arms, and fling the duffle bag over the top. I don't hear an 'ouch' from the other side. So, no guard?

I hop back in the Jeep and Antoinette is laughing. 'Your deadpan is too good. No expression. Just threw it over.'

She takes her foot off the brakes. We roll further down the road, following the fenced-off stream and, behind the stream, the woods. Last time we were here, the trees and bushes that make up these woods were sharply defined by the daylight; I remember little details, like red berries on thickets. Now the woods appear in silhouette, only the treetops making their shape known, against a fast-darkening sky. We reach the point where the fence ends.

As the riverbank runs on, wild bushes take over the task of blocking access to the stream, but there's that narrow gap we spotted last time we were here.

Jumping out, Antoinette helps pull the second duffle bag over my shoulders. Like me, the lanterns and other supplies are too fragile to survive being flung over the gate. They'll have to cross the stream with me.

We cast our eyes down. 'Look how muddy it is,' Antoinette says. The riverbank is the length of two and a half John Safrans, almost straight down. The stream is high and gushing fast, apparently a spring thing – a backlog of precipitation entering the waterways.

Rocks and roots jag out from the bank, here and there, and the plan is that I'll use them for handgrips and footholds. I need to reach a log that has fallen over the stream, which will serve as a bridge. The wild bushes obstruct the ideal point to begin my descent, so I'll have to climb down diagonally. Once there, ten strides should take me across the log and to the other side of the stream.

'Don't bite your nails.' Antoinette knocks my hand from my mouth. 'John, you're like a child. Stop making me be your mother. I can't anymore. I feel sick, saying goodbye to my son.'

'Goodbye, Mother.'

'John. I'm sad, I'm nervous.'

We kiss goodbye.

The climb down quickly becomes more of a controlled slide. With my face pressed against the mud, fingers gripping knots of tree roots, my foot reaches around below me, searching for the log. Intellectually, I know moments ago I scraped my thigh on a jutting rock, but the pain isn't registering yet. I'm in sensory overload – the drizzle, the mud, the exertion, the fear a neighbour will spot us and call the cops. The pain in my thigh is at the back of the queue.

My toes tickle the log. I loosen my grip on the roots, press my palms against the mud, and allow myself to slip down the last little bit, setting my foot on the log. Wriggling my hips, I bring the rest of my body towards the log and set down the other foot. I gently release my palms from the wall and steady myself. Looking up, I find Antoinette leaning over the lip of the bank, preparing to let the first plastic jug of water slide into my arms.

'This is art, you know that?' she says, releasing the jug. '*This*. You slipping down and crossing over and climbing through the woods and squatting. Conceptual art.'

I catch the jug and hold it against the bank with my shin. The drizzle has eased into something heavier; I don't feel like talking about art.

'Your audio recordings are something we could submit for an art prize. Not a book prize. You could win as an artist!'

Jesus Christ. 'The other one, please.'

Antoinette disappears, then returns with the second jug. Something else is now on her mind.

'Will I get cancelled?' she calls down.

'What's that?' I call up.

'Will I get cancelled for being part of this?'

'You're not worried about being arrested – you're worried about being cancelled?'

'This is like a cancellable kind of thing. Breaking into a Black man's house. I mean, you can do it, you're Jewish. But what have I got? Greek?'

As always, I don't know if she's joking, or serious, or joking to make a serious point.

'The water, please.'

The second jug slides down.

With the duffle slung over my back, carrying the water jugs, I start across the log. The stream laps against the wood, forces itself past. The jugs are not the hindrance I expected, instead acting as counterweights, one in each hand. This balancing act just needs to work for ten strides.

As I reach the halfway mark, the sound of the stream, the rain and the wind softens into the background. Moss has taken over this part of the log, and a new sound comes to dominate: the squelch the wood produces each time my shoe comes down. The log is belching, reminding me how slippery and precarious my situation is.

I lose faith. I start teetering forward for the next two, three, four, five strides, struggling with my footing, before finally collapsing to my knees in the mud on the other side.

I'm now faced with getting up the muddy bank on *this* side of the stream. The two jugs, formerly unintrusive counterweights, are now two albatrosses. The drizzle, not that long ago rejuvenating, has become the kind of rain you stay inside to avoid.

It takes me two ungraceful climbs to get the job done, hauling one albatross per trip, but I manage to get myself and all my stuff up the steep ascent. The pain in my thigh has moved to the front of the queue.

I look back to Antoinette.

'There are so many mushrooms,' she offers. 'Don't eat them.'

I disappear into the woods.

THE ENCHANTED FOREST

Not long ago I was seeing these woods as a silhouette from the window of the Jeep. Now I'm enclosed in that silhouette, oak trees shooting up to the sky. Down here, I'm confronted by an anarchy of plants. No path is laid out before me. Tree trunks have collapsed onto bushes. Nothing here has ever faced pruning shears.

I'm deep enough in that I can no longer see the stream, whose path I'm following, although I can still hear it. There's no point going any deeper, further away from the water; if anything, more disorder lies that way.

Stay focused. Just head towards the mansion.

Weeds are tripwires, so I'm lifting my feet high. I mount a log, stretch back to haul up the jugs, then slide down the other side. I keep plodding on. The stream flows freely towards the mansion, mocking me, while all this flora pushes back against me; I'm swimming against the tide.

A branch finds my face, sending my glasses askew. They're an expensive pair and I consider folding them into my pocket, but I worry that without them a twig will take out my eye. I push on.

I see Lord Robert Baden-Powell. Well, I don't *see* him, but he has crawled into my mind. The founder of the Scout movement. There he is. A broom-brush moustache, crow's-feet etched into his face, and a khaki brown Scout hat. Does this make me an artist? I should be focused on where my next step lands, darting my eyes around for danger – worldly concerns – but instead, my imagination has gone on its own hike.

As a little Boy Scout, I trekked through endless miles of forest. So, at first blush, that would seem to explain why this distinguished English gentleman has made his appearance. But my mind hikes further afield. Was Lord Baden-Powell my first Kanye?

Stick with me here. During one of these Scouts outings, hiking through the woods, a fellow cub leant in and said, 'My dad told me Lord Baden-Powell didn't like Jews.' (It turns out he praised Adolf Hitler's book *Mein Kampf*, and dined with the heads of the Hitler Youth.) Was this the first time that I was minding my own business and somebody said something to me about Jews that I found jarring and curious? Something that didn't just poof into thin air once spoken but flittered about my mind, surviving as a wisp.

Back here in Calabasas: are my feet wet, or just cold? I hike on, but other wisps are coming to mind.

'Woah, check this out,' said a classmate in high school, pointing to the upcoming page in Shakespeare. Macbeth is trekking through mud – as I am trekking through mud – and comes across three witches, who have stirred the 'liver of a blaspheming Jew' into a bubbling cauldron. Along with hemlock and yew – poisonous plants – the Jew's organ is needed to conjure the souls of the dead. A blasphemer, the Jew is worthy of being part of the noxious stew because he has not accepted Christ.

In fact, Shakespeare – I'm realising now, another of my Kanyes – twisted his knife deeper into the Jews in *The Merchant of Venice*. There a Jewish moneylender, Shylock, demands a pound of flesh from a Christian merchant who can't pay back a loan.

In Calabasas, dusk has well and truly made way for night. The giant oaks are cutting off any light that the stars and moon might provide. My eyes are straining to find the outline of anything. What was I thinking? I've brought a handheld lantern, a Dolphin torch and a light to strap on my head, but they're all deep in the duffle bag I'm heaving on my back. I'll need a torch to find a torch.

I dig my phone out of my pocket and fumble with my thumbs, activating the flashlight. I hold the light ahead and catch the gloss of a pair of eyes.

My chest tightens. I stand as still as a statue.

My mind tries to deal with the shock, spreading a message throughout my brain and body: *accept the things you cannot change*. But before I can complete a breath, the eyes are nowhere to be seen. Were they even there? If they were indeed eyes, I'm hoping they belonged to an opossum or an owl, something like that. Not a witch.

Meanwhile, it's unambiguous: the damp has seeped through my shoes and socks to my feet. I roll my shoulders, vainly fighting the ache from the weight of the duffle bag. I march on.

Not long after I heard about Shakespeare's venom towards my people, a boy at a party offered, 'You know Walt Disney hated Jews?'

Disney! First the most revered figure in English literature, now the most beloved children's filmmaker. (He welcomed Nazi filmmaker Leni Riefenstahl to Hollywood.)

All these wisps intertwining, floating inside my head since childhood, right through to the man of the hour.

'Kanye isn't a fan!' a friend told me a few months ago, offering a clip where Kanye muses over the Jew: 'They'll take us and milk us until we die.'

The Jew extracting a pound of flesh.

It doesn't end there. This goes deeper and deeper, reaching towards the centre of the earth of me.

As a kid, when these wisps were first being whispered into my ear, I was living with my grandparents. They fled Poland for the Soviet Union in 1939, where they were imprisoned in a work camp – a forest in northern Russia – where trees were chopped down and milled. They were the only ones left standing in their families; parents, siblings, cousins, uncles and aunts, all had been extinguished back in Poland.

If you reckon Jews go on about the Holocaust too much, you should have been in my grandparents' lounge room – they never spoke about it. And you knew not to bring it up.

These wisps swirling around my head are a strange beast: ethereal, esoteric, aesthetically seductive. Irresistible juxtapositions of good and evil. Cubs, cherub-faced and innocent, contrasting with Lord Baden-Powell dining with Nazis. In my mind, right now as I pull myself over another log, their little pink faces press against a window, watching Lord Baden-Powell and Hitler's men devouring their meal, teeth tearing through meat. And now a translucent

THE ENCHANTED FOREST

image of Walt Disney, his arm around Leni Riefenstahl, overlaps another image, this one of Disney with his arm around Snow White.

These woods feel like an enchanted forest. I half-expect Bambi to poke his nose out from behind a shrub.

Taking all this in, I realise I'd be short-changing myself if I justified this trespassing as nihilistic thrill-seeking. If I wanted that, I'd train surf. No. Kanye is playing with my family story for his art. He started it.

I realise Antoinette was right after all. This adventure is art.

The enchanted forest opens, and there stands Kanye's mansion.

THE GIANT HAND

Suddenly soaked, in the dead of night, I realise that the oak trees have actually been sheltering me from a downpour. As well as the sound of the driving rain, there's a loud pitter-pattering. Where's that coming from? It sounds like fingers tapping on a desk, but massively amplified. I was already terror-struck, and now the image of a giant hand has entered my head.

I walk downhill from the woods, not too far, and reach a patio. I don't need to scale a fence or wall to gain access. Instead, I need to jump *down* onto the brick patio. The drop is about my height if my head was sawn off.

I rest the two jugs on the lip of the muddy slope and leap.

When I land, squeaking on a puddle, I can feel my ankles jarring. The jugs tip over and fall from the lip above, smashing onto the bricks of the patio, plastic bursting open, the clean water intermingling with the puddles. I wince.

I look about and decide not to get grumpy – it's not like there's a shortage of water at this place.

I pull off the duffle bag and roll my shoulders. The patio offers entry to the mansion through a set of sliding glass doors, but shutters block me from peeking in. I need to take a moment to orient myself.

Stepping out of the woods, I was already too close to the mansion to take it in properly. And now I'm even closer. So, what *can* I make out? A trough, I'm guessing for watering horses, is tipped on its side on the patio. The rain plays it like a steel drum. A large metal chest, full of gardening tools, has found its way here too.

The neighbour across the street, Ernie, said Kanye had wrapped the mansion in white plastic to form a protective bubble. Time and weather have had their way. The scaffolding remains, metal poles pitched into the earth around the patio, travelling all the way up, past the tip of the mansion's rooftop. But an enormous white plastic sheet, formerly stretched across two poles, now hangs limply from one.

Scraps of white plastic, the size of picnic rugs, have torn themselves away from the scaffolding at different points around the mansion. They are now wrapped around tree trunks and twisted on the ground of the woods I just emerged from, illuminated, but only barely, by the night sky. And now it comes together. The rain striking these plastic sheets is responsible for what I've been hearing – fingers tapping on a desk, amplified. Even knowing this, the picture of the giant hand won't leave my mind.

Revelations are coming at me in the wrong order. The moment I left the woods and took in the rear of the mansion, I should have realised there was a reason I could make out the patio. A reason I could see the tipped-over trough and, looking down, my own muddy shoes. A light is glowing here on the patio.

Why is there a light on? A sign of life is usually a good thing, but not now, not here. The light fitting is designed to look like a Victorian-era streetlamp, its wrought-iron stem screwed into the wall.

Let me think this through. Ernie the neighbour told me that a few weeks ago the guards left for the last time. Did they forget to switch off the light? Or did they not even know the light was on? Has it been glowing for much longer, Kanye failing to flick it off when he left? That was over a year ago.

I'm both overthinking the angles and dodging the real question. Is someone in the mansion right now?

My fortune-cookie wisdom – *accept the things you cannot change* – is not calming me down. I realise that, for the week leading up to this moment, I've been preparing myself for the fear of living at an *abandoned* mansion. But what if someone is here? A guard? A homeless man like James?

There's one other potential resident to consider. James's cardboard sign said Kanye has gone missing, and articles in the press have said the same. Some lawyer was trying to serve him with papers but had to give up.

Is Kanye hiding away here?

The Scouts' motto is 'Be Prepared' – it was emblazoned on my cub belt buckle. I should have been, but I'm not.

There were no guards here one week ago. That's the salient point, isn't it? *One week ago.* Why didn't I check with Ernie, one hour ago? Get an update on the situation. For all I know, a week back some other neighbour alerted Kanye's people, or the real-estate agent, that they spotted two busybodies in a Jeep lurking around the mansion gate, and the guards were called back in.

Or how about this: ninety-minutes ago, a woman across the street, watching her soaps, hops off her couch and heads for the fridge. Passing by the window, across the street she sees a man flinging a duffle bag over the mansion gate. She pulls out her phone and calls ... who?

Kanye's other neighbour, Gregg, told me people in the street have called the sheriff on him for cranking his tractor engine too early on a Sunday morning. Is the sheriff here? Is he digging through my duffle bag right now, in Kanye's kitchen or dining room? If someone saw me throw the bag over the fence, it would be the first thing law enforcement look for.

I squat down and zip open the duffle bag I carried with me. I paw through the lamps, first-aid kit and bear repellent. Oh hell. No, no, no, no, no. I packed my *passport* in the other bag. In this scenario, the sheriff finds the smokiest gun of all smoking guns: my identity papers.

There's nothing for it but to face the music. The handle on the sliding door leading inside looks to be standard fare: a keyhole and lever to flick down. I give it a fidget, knowing there's not a chance the door is unlocked.

Except it is.

The lever clicks. I squeak the doors ever so slightly apart, only the width of my nose, although I don't dare lean that nose in. Darkness fills the gap. Is the fact that this door is unlocked connected to the light out here being switched on? Did someone come out to the patio for a cigarette? Antoinette would know if Kanye smokes, but she's not here. I'm in the worst of both worlds: I'm alone, but not necessarily on my own.

I was on autopilot squeaking those doors apart. Muscle memory from all the sliding doors I've faced over my life. I stopped at the width of my nose because that's when it kicked in: anything could be on the other side. Could Kanye be waiting for me with a cocked pistol? The sheriff could. What are the gun laws in Calabasas?

I take a breath and contemplate the situation, which is hard to do when the rain won't shut up. If someone is standing in the room, they've just seen the doors inch apart. They know I'm here. I've passed the point of no return. As such, I squeak the doors apart further, the width of my skull.

'Hello?'

I lean that very skull into the mansion. Craning my neck back and forth, I find no one to return my salutation.

My eyes adjust and I make out a keyboard on a stand, its power cable snaking across the floor to a socket in the wall. I'm so frightened, it might as well be an actual snake.

Otherwise empty, the room itself is striking. From outside, the mansion looked to be two storeys. Going by this room, it's one, with a ceiling so high you could rent it out to circus acrobats. The walls, ceiling and floor are all painted the same hue of blue. I'm not sure I've ever seen a room enclosed in one solid colour. Through a large archway to my left, another room, as far as I can make out, is also blue from top to tail. A different archway, straight ahead, leads to what looks to be a blue hallway.

Again, I'm too slow to pick up on important things. The only reason I'm dealing with blueness, not blackness, is that there's a blade of light coming from somewhere up that hallway, granting a little illumination.

Slipping through the glass doors, two further meek hellos escape my lips. By the time I've reached the hallway, I'm holding myself steady, like before lifting weights, fearing that otherwise I'll collapse. I try to convince myself to underthink, to not take in how dangerous this could be. Okay, I'm overthinking underthinking.

I poke my head around the corner. The hallway runs both ways.

'Hello?'

I bite the bullet and leave the, erm, 'safety' of the archway.

'Hello?'

Heading left down the hallway, away from the light, I soon reach a door that's swung open. A skylight allows in a faint glow. The walls and ceiling within this empty room are also blue, but, unlike elsewhere, it's not a coat of paint, it's foam padding, presumably installed for acoustics. This must be a recording studio, although there is no equipment here now. But, considering my state of mind, perhaps I should walk in, shut the door behind me and use it as a padded cell.

I slink on. I find half-a-dozen more blue rooms, painted not padded, coming off this hallway. I don't know the architect's intent for each room; they're empty except for boxes and other odds and ends – an empty bookshelf on its side, a couple of rolled-up rugs. But each could comfortably be a bedroom holding a king-size bed.

I can't tell if the hallway *really* is bending and the walls are different heights, giving a slope to the ceiling, or if it just looks like that in the inadequate light.

A final door, swung open at the end of the hall, reveals a blue bathroom. The toilet isn't abiding by the colour scheme – it's sparkling silver.

Having reached the end of the road I turn around and head towards the light. 'Hello?'

Retracing my steps, I pass the archway where I entered this hallway. I left the sliding doors open, so I can still hear both the rain and the giant hand tapping on the desk. I notice my soggy shoelaces need tying but decide to just keep going.

I reach a corner where the hallway turns sharply left. When I crook my head around the corner, white light overwhelms. Lit up from above by fluorescent tubes, I find myself in a long tunnel, constructed from scaffolding and white plastic.

'Hello?'

I step further into the wormhole. Soon, on my right, an archway leads to the largest blue room I've come across yet. It could fit my whole house. A leather executive chair is parked behind an impressive wooden desk. Nearby, a bucket is accepting a drip from the ceiling. The room is otherwise empty. Thanks to the light radiating from the wormhole, I can make out the blue more clearly: it's the shade of Donald Duck's sailor cap. (It seems Walt Disney, who jumped into my head in the woods, is still there.)

'Hello?'

I leave this room for later and thread further down the glowing wormhole. It finally leads me back outside, through the front door of the mansion. Or rather, where the front door would be if there wasn't a wormhole in its place.

The rain hits my face. I'm on the flipside. Ninety minutes ago, I stood out on the road, the fence blocking my view of the mansion. Now I'm inside and that same fence blocks me from seeing the road.

Yes, I'm on the flipside, but I might as well be inside out and upside down too. This feels very odd. Odd without precedent. I'm overseas, I'm out of range. I'm standing in Kanye West's front yard. I can feel it in my skin; these aren't just goosebumps of fear, they're goosebumps of oddness. The moon looks down upon this farce. If I was up there lounging on a crater, it would hardly be a stranger situation than the one I'm in down here.

My wet shoes are suctioned to the concrete. The front grounds, large enough to assemble an army, spread out before me. It's all concrete. A line of trees in enormous white pots, taller than the mansion, breaks only where a bridge leads to the front gate. If the sheriff is somewhere, he's not holding my duffle bag; I can make it out, resting right where I flung it over the gate.

I sprint through the downpour. Arriving on the bridge, slipping as I skid to a halt, I hear a familiar sound. Looking down over the metal railing, there it is: the gushing stream.

I grab the duffle bag by the gate and shoot back over the bridge. As I run, from the corner of my eye I catch that there is more than concrete to the front grounds. To the left of the mansion, there's a huge garage and a separate two-storey house. To the right, the concrete ends and a green paddock takes over. No time to think about that now. I escape into the wormhole, reach the blue room, the one with the desk and the executive chair, turn in, and collapse.

A QUICK STAB

The sound of static – a quick stab – comes from somewhere. Freaked out, I look around. A white square is screwed to a blue wall. Could that be a speaker? It could also be an air vent.

A second stab of static.

Of course! The walkie-talkie.

I reach into my pocket. 'Hello? Oh my God. Hey, it's John here. How are you? Over. Can you hear me?'

'Put the volume up. Over.'

I tell Antoinette I'm in a giant blue room and the lights are working in the wormhole, so there must be electricity.

'Great news. Over.'

I make my way to the desk and leather chair, the only furnishings in the room, aside from the bucket collecting rainwater.

'There's all this mail,' I tell Antoinette, shuffling through envelopes I find on the desk. 'I'm trying to see when the last one's stamped. December 2022. Water bill. Okay, now I'm going to see if there's water.'

On the other side of this room from the wormhole, another archway. I step through and am dazzled by an industrial kitchen. Some of the light from the wormhole makes it all the way here. The kitchen is also blue, punctuated by silver appliances: multiple stoves and ovens, multiple fridges, multiple dishwashers. A pizza oven that could accommodate the world's largest pepperoni pizza.

'I'm walking through a very clean kitchen,' I report. 'Very clean stainless steel. I was really hoping it'd be a bit dustier.'

Dust would signal this kitchen has been abandoned for a while, which would grant me a sense of safety. Dust would be a sign that I'm alone in this mansion. But it isn't dusty.

'There's some food here, too.'

Lining a shelf: bottles of cooking oil, jars of pasta and tins of chocolate milk. The pans hanging from the wall look like a planetary chart.

'Okay, I'm going to turn the tap.' I approach a sink, which is sized somewhere between a normal sink and a bathtub. 'Oh no. That tap, no water. But, yeah, there's definitely electricity. I'll find another tap.'

I pop about all the sinks in this massive kitchen, twisting the taps. Nothing.

'I'll drive down the street,' Antoinette says. 'And see what the range is on this walkie-talkie.'

'How far away are you now?'

'I'm outside the compound.'

Her referring to the mansion as a compound makes me think: Kanye is eccentric and driven enough, he *could* conceivably assemble an army on the front grounds. And, now that the thought has taken me, he could train them in the woods behind the place. Yes, this man with grievances against the Jews could do that.

'I'll drive out,' says Antoinette. 'I'll drive to the McDonald's and give it a go.'

The box the walkie-talkies came in promised a range of thirty-five miles. Antoinette makes it half a mile, to the top of the road, before they stop functioning. Electric hissing overtakes her voice.

She drives back into range and we nut out a plan. She says she'll return at six in the morning.

'Over.'

'Over.'

'Over.'

An archway from the kitchen leads to a walk-in pantry, a room of its own, which, like everywhere else around here, is blue with an impossibly high ceiling. A ladder leans against a wall, which makes sense, because the highest pantry shelves are not far from that ceiling.

Flicking the light on, I'm awestruck by a spectrum of colours: over a hundred oversized jars of spices, each labelled. Aniseed Star, Cardamom Brown Pods, Nutmeg, Cinnamon Bark, Asafoetida (no clue what that is but it's yellow), Juniper Berries, Sumac, Amchur, Annatto, Anardana, Byadgi Chile, Urfa Biber Chile, Korean Chili, Nigella Sativa, Sichuan Peppercorns, Galangal. On and on it goes, green, red, purple, orange. The jars are neatly arranged, evenly spaced. The vibrant colours are a respite from the madness of this mansion's endless blue.

However, my calmness does not last. Turning my head, I catch something in my line of sight that startles me more than those eyes in the woods. One jar, and only one jar in the entire pantry, has its own shelf. There it sits on an otherwise empty bottom plank.

    Saffron.

SYNCHRONICITY

This memory only took up one second of my headspace, standing in the pantry, but I need to slow it down to explain.

One night, years ago, driving to work in Melbourne, I spotted a man by a tram stop on a busy city road, stumbling in and out of traffic. Rain was pelting down and cars were honking at the man.

I pulled over and soon detected that he was a little eccentric. He told me he needed to get to a house nearby. I was early for work so didn't mind offering him a lift. Yeah, yeah, I know you shouldn't pick up strangers, but what pushed me across the line was his affliction. He had what doctors call kyphosis. But I'm not a doctor, so I only knew a more matter-of-fact term. This man was a hunchback.

He didn't know the address of the house he needed to get to, but said he could direct me. Except it quickly became apparent that he suffered from poor sight; from what I could tell, he was nearly blind. So I read out street signs as we approached intersections and he instructed me – left, right, straight ahead.

Not long into this journey, I slowed down and stopped for our first red light. The man asked what landmarks were about, so he could determine how close we were to his destination. Glancing out the window, I couldn't believe it. I had to blink to make sure I wasn't imagining things. Written in big letters across the most prominent building at this intersection: Hunchbax Theatre Restaurant.

Regaining my composure, I described every building in the vicinity except for the theatre restaurant, with its vampire bats, monsters and, yes, a hunchback, painted across its facade.

The light turned green and I took off, and a while later I successfully dropped the man off at his destination.

Later I told a colleague: how is this not proof of God, or the hand of some mystical force? How is it possible that I pick up a stranger, and he turns out to be a hunchback, and at our first red light he asks what's out the window and it's Hunchbax Theatre Restaurant?

My friend said I was overreacting, that in the field of psychology there is a theory called synchronicity. As he explained it, our minds thirst for patterns, so we notice connections and then inflate their importance, ignoring the countless moments in our lives that don't form patterns. The law of probability dictates that, with millions of moments washing over us, we can cherrypick this and that, make a link, and decide that it's beyond rational explanation. To him, what I was reading as supernatural was perfectly explicable by probability and the science of the mind.

I mean, I get where he's coming from, but come on. I picked up a hunchback and not five minutes later we're outside Hunchbax Theatre Restaurant.

Years later, at a party, I found a book on synchronicity on the host's bookshelf. And according to the book, my colleague had it all wrong! The father of the theory of synchronicity, Carl Jung, *did* think that what we dismiss as coincidence could be signs of the paranormal, messages sent to us in a manner science is yet to grasp.

So the theatre restaurant could have held meaning. And so could the jar of saffron in Kanye's mansion. Yes, maybe whoever stacked these shelves was left with one straggling jar and it just happened to be the spice assigned the Arabic word that is the root word of my family name, Safran. But standing here, a dog barking in the distance breaking through the violence of the rain, it doesn't feel like a coincidence.

THE DRIP

The big blue room, with its desk, office chair and bucket accepting a drip, now holds one more item. An Australian cocooned in a sleeping bag.

The ceiling is vaulted, two sides sloping up, meeting at a beam in the centre. Lying face up, this is not what I think of when I think of a ceiling. This is two tic-tac-toe boards of skylights either side of the central beam. But there's no perspex in these skylights, instead a sheet of transparent plastic struggles to keep the elements out. A build-up of leaves, branches, acorns and sludge pushes down and distends each square.

The bucketing rain stresses each square further, and the sheets of plastic can only do so much; water drips in around the perimeter of the room. I've positioned myself underneath the thick wooden beam in the centre of the ceiling, where no leaky square should get me.

I hate this. Or, rather, I want this to be over. I want it to be tomorrow morning already. I'm not having fun. The sound of rain pelting concrete echoes up the wormhole. It sounds so much like approaching footsteps that I'm talking to it.

'Hello?'

In an effort to calm down, I'm bending the notion of 'the law of probability' to breaking point, telling myself: 'The law of probability dictates there's probably no one else on this property.' What does that even mean? All I'm doing is throwing a science term into a soup of nonsense.

For one, another house sits on this property, right next to the mansion. I spotted it as I sprinted from the bridge back into the wormhole.

'Screw this blue mansion and its leaking roof,' Kanye could have said, wheeling his Balenciaga travel bag from the wormhole to that house.

Is he sleeping there right now?

Through the storm comes a monstrous crack, a finger bone breaking in the giant hand.

THE NEXT MORNING: DAY ONE IN THE MANSION

My eyes snap open. It's the same room, but things look very different. For a start, there's light. A set of frosted windows allows in the pre-dawn light, but only the vaguest of shapes in the grounds out the front.

But the headline news is not the light but what this light reveals. Mushrooms line the skirting boards of this room. I didn't catch them last night, with shadows cast everywhere.

I shed my sleeping bag and crouch to examine them. For all I know, these are toadstools, not mushrooms. Some are cream, some are orange, others are brown with white sprinkles, like lamingtons. Some cross the line beyond yellow and look to be gold. They run the perimeter of the room, squeezing through gaps where the floor meets the walls, along with the green grassy veins of weeds. The leaking roof must be their watering can. The woods are starting to eat the house.

The floor is blue foam, the type installed at playgrounds that have gone woke, no longer allowing kids to crack open their skulls on bare concrete. I squish my bare toes on the foam, enjoying the tickling sensation.

Despite the soft floor, my body has paid a toll for sleeping on the ground last night. To soothe a cramp in my neck, I give it a stretch, turning my head. The wall on the far side of the room comes into my line of vision. I stop squishing my toes. Unease washes over me.

A Bible passage, chalked in white, sits in the middle of the wall. I calm myself, remembering Bible passages were on the walls of the schoolhouse, too. This one reads:

> *The LORD set Ezekiel down in the valley of bones*
> *The LORD said 'O dry bones, I will lay sinew and stretch skin*
>   *over you'*
> *And, the bones came clattering together*
> *And they stood up on their feet, a very, very great army*

I know this one. God was telling Ezekiel that the Jewish people will find themselves scattered, not united as a community. Feeling spiritually dead. And they will think God has abandoned them. But He hasn't. Because just when the Jews have lost hope, God will bring them back together. And, to show Ezekiel He's not just full of hot air and He can actually do this, God assembled a pile of bones into skeletons, stretched skin over the bones, and breathed life into them, creating a Jewish army.

It's too much to absorb. My brain is struggling to pick a starting point out of the multiple candidates.

DAY ONE IN THE MANSION

Why, last night, did I ponder the possibility of Kanye assembling an army on the grounds of the mansion, and now, here's a Bible passage about God raising an army? *Synchronicity?*

When we met James, the schoolhouse squatter, he assured me the Bible quotes on the walls were by Kanye's hand. I wonder how Kanye chooses the passages he does. More specifically, why he chose this one – it's explicitly pro-Jewish. It says God is going to stand by the Jews.

KANYE AND THE TORAH

Four days earlier, I spoke to Tamar, an educational consultant. Her voice was soothing to me, reminiscent of the Jews I squawked with back home, despite her American accent. I had been seeking her out for a while and she finally returned my calls.

'I was called by a lawyer, and I should say: Jewish Orthodox lawyer. And I get these calls all the time. They wanted to see if I wanted to help a brand-new school.'

The brand-new school was Kanye West's Donda Academy. Kanye, or someone in his circle, wanted it accredited like a conventional school, and getting schools up to code for accreditation was one of Tamar's specialties.

'I didn't know him. I don't listen to his music. I don't know anything about him.'

She said yes to the gig.

'I met the principal and the assistant principal, took a tour around the school, and saw how they needed much, much more than what I was hired to do.'

'What seemed to be lacking?' I asked.

'Everything. My first meeting, I say, "I don't even think the building you're in is kosher for a school."'

By unkosher, she didn't mean pigs were trotting about the playground.

'My friend who's a real estate broker does a title search and, lo and behold, the building is only zoned for heavy industrial work.'

This was a later incarnation of the Donda Academy than the one Antoinette and I had snooped about in, the one in the woods of Simi Valley. Kanye had another go of it, in a semi-industrial area of Los Angeles called Northridge.

Tamar spotted other unkosher items on the menu.

'I talked with the principal. What's your math curriculum? "We don't have one." What's your English curriculum? "We don't have one." What's your history curriculum? "We don't have one."'

She refused to meet Kanye.

'Everything that I did was through messages to the lawyer, to Kanye, and back to me. I knew that if I spoke with him, he would never agree to what I needed to do to get that school functioning.' She felt his decisions regarding the school were impulsive and he couldn't be reasoned with. 'He went to a basketball game. He met this guy, they somehow hit it off, and he makes him another assistant principal. And this guy was a total doofus. I mean, one of the most idiotic people I've ever seen.'

She said there was a rule that Kanye's circle lived by. 'Whenever he said he wanted something to happen, you waited twenty-four hours. Because you knew that he was crazy. He might change his mind.'

Despite her refusal to talk to him face to face, she was now one of the people in his circle.

'I'm in the car driving with my husband and I get a call from the principal, and she's hysterical. Kanye wants to fly the entire school to Paris for fashion week. A hundred and fifty kids.' These children would be singing in a choir, as part of Kanye's fashion show. 'Now, you've got to understand, a lot of these kids have never travelled, don't have a passport. I said, "Chill, it's only Tuesday. They're not scheduled to fly until Friday. Twenty-four-hour rule!"'

Kanye didn't change his mind. Although he did agree to scale things down.

'The principal calls me back. "We're only taking fifty kids." Like that's much more manageable?!' I could hear her rolling her eyes over the phone.

'So she comes to my house: $997,000 to charter a jet – a 747. Lawyers have to get passports for all the kids. And then you have to get hotel rooms in Paris. The only hotel available was the five-star InterContinental. And, of course, he flies there alone on his jet. Kim Kardashian flies on her jet. They sang one song and came back home.'

But Tamar thought, hey, it was his money. She stayed focused on the goings-on back in Northridge, Los Angeles.

'He wanted it to be a Christian military school.'

Damn. I mean, Donda Academy was catering to children from

kindergarten through to grade five. What would be the syllabus at such an institution?

'Well, his first idea was to shave all the kids' heads.'

Tamar's madcap story about the Paris fashion show already had me overexcited; this revelation left me reeling. Back at the Simi Valley schoolhouse, when I read the word 'compound' on the sketchpad, I had visions of Kanye training a militia. Back then you could have dismissed me as suffering from an overactive imagination. But since coming to LA I've also heard rumours that Kanye wanted to give the kids assault-weapon training by fifth grade. If anything, I hadn't been thinking wildly enough!

Out of the 150-odd students at Donda Academy, most were Black or Hispanic, and all bar one was Christian. The one outlier? A kid from a Jewish family.

'The mother said she woke up one morning and God spoke to her and said she had to serve Ye.'

This attitude was typical among the families that sent their kids to the school. For them, Kanye – with his talent, charisma, money and celebrity – was sprinkled with magic dust. They wanted in on his world, no matter what.

'It dawned on me. They're not speaking out on how bonkers the school is, even for their own children's sake. They don't care that their kids are learning nothing.'

Then came the week Kanye made his views on Jews clear, publicly glorifying Adolf Hitler. The 'doofus' Kanye had met at a basketball game and hired as an assistant principal called up Tamar.

'He goes, "Listen, Tamar, I've had a really rough week." And I said, "Woah, woah, woah, woah. *You've* had a rough week? Do you know what my week's been like with all the antisemitism?" And he just pretends I didn't even say that. And it was at that moment that I realised I was done. That was it.'

The scales fell from her eyes. She realised Kanye's public outburst that week wouldn't have been the first time he had spoken that way about Jewish people. He must have been like this in private and his circle had chosen to keep that side of him secret from Tamar.

Indeed, NBC news discovered in 2022 that 'six people who have worked with Ye or witnessed him in professional settings over the past five years said they had heard him praise Adolf Hitler or mention conspiracy theories about Jewish people'. In fact, Kanye paid a settlement to a former employee who complained about his antisemitism.

'The school had a pastor, and I had gotten close to him,' Tamar said. 'They're all preaching peace and everything else that good Christian people preach. And not one person said anything to me. They all knew I was Jewish.'

So in the end it wasn't so much Kanye's advocacy for Nazis, it was the cover-up by those around him that truly wounded Tamar.

But what Tamar said next stopped me in my tracks.

'There was a rabbi I knew who was studying Torah with Kanye every week. An Orthodox Jewish one.'

The Torah, and some additional scripture, makes up the Bible for the Jews. Christians take all this and add on the story of Jesus Christ for their Bible.

'Who was this rabbi?' I spluttered, unable to contain my excitement. 'Was it a particular synagogue?'

I was picturing Kanye leaning over a Torah scroll, running over the Hebrew with a silver pointer shaped like a human hand, like I did on my bar mitzvah.

'I'm not going to say, because I'm not going to give away his information at all. It's not mine to give away.'

'Fair enough,' I said. Over the phone, she couldn't see my pout.

DEM BONES

Drip, drip, drip, drip. The bucket accepting the drip isn't helping me focus on the Bible passage chalked on the wall. And I do want to focus on it. Because – did Kanye learn this story of God raising bones from his Torah class? And why is a man so invested in dissing Jews drawn to Jews in the first place?

I guess he could have turned up to the rabbi's class to acquire the secrets of the Jewish scripture. That he intuited they were evil, but he wanted to gather the evidence to help him make his case against the Jews. I've witnessed this technique. At a neo-Nazi rally in Australia, a gentleman in a balaclava approached me, quoting what he insisted were wicked passages from Jewish scripture and . . .

Listen, can we get to this later? I can't concentrate right now. And it's not just the drip – it's knowing that Kanye could be asleep, or brewing coffee, in the two-storey house next to this mansion. What's up with that place?

I check my watch. I've got time before the scheduled walkie-talkie call with Antoinette, so I decide to go poke around outside.

Three structures stand before me. From right to left, there's the mansion, a large garage and the two-storey house. Through the shreds of dilapidated white plastic dangling from the scaffolding, I can see all three look like ranches. A non-American would sooner imagine these buildings in Texas than California, but they abide by the architectural flavour of the street.

The garage and the two-storey house have gabled roofs, which remind me of barns. For all I know, waiting behind the wooden panels of these two buildings are chickens, not Kanye.

Along the mansion's roof, three dormer windows imply three attics. But, as far as I can tell, these are decorative and there are no attics. Exploring the house, I couldn't see anything leading into the roof. But now that I think about it, I'm not 100 per cent sure this is the case.

My gaze turns to the garage. Its door is tilted fully open, so I can see that there are no vehicles inside, just boxes and shiny tools hanging on the walls: shovels, bolt-cutters, wrenches, saws, drills and hammers. Just like it seemed someone had stocked every spice in the world in the pantry, seemingly the garage holds every tool in the world.

Two matte-black vehicles are parked out front of the garage. The beads of water left from last night's downpour have defeated the matte effect, shining up the paintwork, even on this overcast morning.

One is an all-terrain vehicle, a Polaris RZR. It looks skeletal (more bones!). Its roll cage (rib cage!) isn't just a safety feature but the aesthetic upon which the rest of the vehicle is based: chunky tyres connected to big suspension springs, no windows, not even a windscreen.

In contrast, the other vehicle parked here is a panic room on wheels. Badged SHERP, it's an intimidating black box, the tyres almost as tall as I am. The tinted windows are as dark as its black metal panels. Lacking a nose, the engine must be tucked away somewhere else.

During my stay, I discover four more RZRs and one more SHERP on the grounds. These are both military vehicles. While the US Army is a client for the RZR, the Ukrainian Army buys the SHERP. I guess if Kanye raises his army, they'll have something to drive.

Dodging puddles, I make my way from the garage to the two-storey house. I hold my nerve and knock on the door. It's a firm knock, eliciting an echo.

Nothing.

The street is so quiet, I fear the neighbours heard that, so I chicken out of a follow-up knock. Instead, I gingerly turn the golden doorknob. It's unlocked. I guess when trespassing requires fording a stream, a homeowner is relaxed about locking their door.

I begin pushing the door open and, through the crack, in the darkness, catch a frightening sight. A person seated on the floor, up against a wall. I recoil and pull the door shut.

I feel like falling to pieces, but I've snookered myself. I can flee back to the blue mansion, but this person will still be here. And now they know *I'm* here. I've reached another point of no return.

I muster up the courage and take another peek through the crack.

'Hello, sorry, my name is John. I'm a writer, but not paparazzi.'

I've picked that up from Antoinette. She's been adding 'we're not paparazzi' when I approach people.

'I'm not a thief,' I say.

They don't budge.

'I don't have a gun. Hello?'

Something's wrong. Nausea rushes through me. Are they dead?

I push the door open all the way and the morning light behind me begins to give form to the contents of the room. My brain is struggling to keep up with what my eyes are letting in. The whole ground floor is one big room. What look to be rag dolls, the size of people, are piled up in the centre. Scattered around this pyramid, reaching all four corners of the room, are more of these creatures, some propped up against the wall. One of these is what I had thought was a dead body.

I breathe. I know what this is. It's art.

And it makes sense. Rich people buy art.

These rag dolls are the size of people, but they're not quite people, they're a creature in between a human and an orangutan. They lack necks but possess arms that dangle to their toes. Teddy-bear ears poke up from their heads. Still, they look more monkey than bear to me. Their skin is canvas, cream coloured.

The room is not blue. An opening cut into the wall, up the back, reveals the first steps of a staircase. My eyes have now adjusted to this dimly lit madness and I can't find anything but dolls. Lacking facial features, I can't tell which side of these creatures is the front. As such, they possess either short tails or long penises.

KANYE AND THE PIT OF BONES

I don't know which artist created and piled up these creatures, but was it meant to evoke US troops discovering pits of Jewish bodies after World War II? That's what it makes me think of in the moment, but am I bringing too much of myself to the pit?

It's not that deep, bro. You're not the main character, Jew. Sometimes a pyramid of rag dolls is just a cigar.

Okay, okay, John, let's go along with your line of thinking. The artist was evoking pits of corpses in war time. Why not Cambodians or Palestinians, narcissist?

I agree! I can prove nothing, in the forensic sense. But, after all of this was over, after I fled the mansion and flew back to Australia, I stumbled upon a data point that suggested Kanye was drawn to art about Jews.

A Melbourne gallery owner told me that, a few years back, Kanye's people had called her up. One of her artists, Kathy Temin, the child of a Holocaust survivor, had built structures covered in synthetic fur. Kathy was grappling with her family history; one of these installations, a white forest with trees shaped in oddball ways, was inspired by the landscape outside Nazi concentration camps she had visited.

Kanye had seen pictures of this white forest on the internet. (What had he been googling? What search terms had led him down this rabbit hole? 'Installation art' or 'Holocaust'?) He wanted Kathy to assemble this forest in one of his Los Angeles mansions. (Not the one I'm presently freaking out at.)

The white forest was to serve as decorations for his and Kim Kardashian's celebrity Christmas party. So Kathy flew out and turned that mansion into a winter wonderland. Kim posted at the time on Instagram: 'Love seeing this decor. Very Dr. Seuss Grinch vibes.'

So, given that Kanye has previously shown interest in Jewish art about the Holocaust, it actually wasn't the maddest thought that a pile of ragdolls represented a pit of Jews.

THE STAIRCASE

I step over another possibly Jewish near-orangutan and reach the foot of the staircase.

'Hello?'

The wooden steps produce the creaking sound of a man much fatter than me making his way up. Soon, the staircase twists.

'Hello?'

I reach the second storey. Another room, also not blue, takes up this entire floor. A king-size bed is pushed against the wall that faces the street. From the window above this bed, I can look down to the black military vehicles, but also across the road to Ernie's house with the big wooden crucifix out front.

A menagerie of musical instruments – drums, guitars, bells, tambourines – is stacked on one side of the room. Perhaps because I'm a writer, I'm more drawn to a sheet of paper taped to a door on the other side of the room.

I make my way over, trying to figure out if the handwriting

on this sheet of paper matches that of the Bible quote in the blue mansion. I reckon it does. Although that is white chalk while this is black Sharpie.

It reads: *'SECURITY TEAM IT IS ONLY ME AND ME ONLY USING THIS REST-ROOM. CLEAN AFTER YOURSELF!! URINE OR POOP OFF SEATS!!!'*

I open the door to a spacious – and clean – bathroom. It seems the security team has abided by the instructions on the note.

Turning back to the room, I might have underestimated things, calling the bed king-size. Is there a size larger than that? Pope-size?

Another note is taped up on the windowsill above the bed.

'SECURITY TEAM NO NAPS OR LAYING ON MY BED!!!'

Well, someone has been lying here – the silk sheets are a little rumpled.

A porcelain cup rests on the bedside table and an open bottle of sake sits on the wooden floor nearby. I walk across and bend over to pick up the bottle.

'Hey!' comes a cry from somewhere in the room.

Jesus Christ!

Panicked, I look around. I realise it's the walkie-talkie that has come to life.

'Hey! John! I havzz an Egg McMuffinzz. Over.'

Antoinette sounds fuzzier than last night; the signal, already not great, is worse.

I look out the window and, from all the way up here, spot what looks to be a matchbox-car Jeep pull up near the gate. From the driver's-side window, a presumed Egg McMuffin flies out, arcs over the gate, and lands on the bridge. The Jeep U-turns and takes off up the road.

Safely away from the mansion, Antoinette's back on the walkie-talkie, eager to find out what things look like behind the gate. I tell her that everything inside the mansion is blue.

'And, on the wall in the mansion, he's got the dry bones story from Ezekiel in the valley of death.'

'Zeekle? What?' she says. 'Please repeat. Over.'

'In the Bible. There's a story where Ezekiel's in the valley of death and there's all these dry bones lying around everywhere. And then God does this miracle where the bones start snapping together and they form all these skeletons and then flesh grows over all the skeletons, and, yeah. So it's like, I don't know. It's like Michael Jackson's "Thriller".'

'John, slow down. You're talking too fast. Over.'

But there's a point I want to make, something I've been chewing over.

'Okay. So this is my point. There's this negro spiritual, this Black American song, really old, and it's: "Dem bones, dem bones, dem dry bones, Hear the word of the Lord! The knee bone connected to the thigh bone, the thigh bone connected to the hip bone, the hip bone connected to the backbone..." That's the bones clattering together, assembling into skeletons!'

'John, you need to talk slower,' Antoinette pleads. 'Over.'

I slow right down.

'It's Black American songwriters who did the song, but it's based on a Jewish Torah story. So, my point being that Kanye is like, oh, Jews leach off Black American culture for profit. But here's an example of Black Americans and they've culturally appropriated – they've vampired – the Jewish Torah. You know what I mean?'

She doesn't know what I mean.

'So, it's like, this is Black people stealing from the Jews. So where does that fit in with Kanye saying the Jews are always stealing off the Blacks?'

Antoinette has cracked up laughing. And even through the fuzz, I can tell she's laughing at me, not with me.

'Fine. You've won. Checkmate, Kanye West!' she says, dripping with sarcasm.

'I think it's a good argument. How's that not a good argument?'

She thinks my whole premise is in poor taste.

'I don't know the history of African American music,' she says. 'On the cotton fields, it might have been one of those slave songs. That one of Kanye's ancestors might've sung.'

How has this turned against me? This all made sense in my head. In my head, I *did* win.

What is Antoinette trying to say, anyway? What's her counterpoint?

'What's your dad's name?' she asks.

'Alex.'

'Culturally appropriated from the Greeks. That's my people. You sound crazy, John.' She laughs again. 'I think you need to drink more water.'

This is infuriating. I've been misunderstood! I don't care that Black Americans have taken Torah stories, I care that . . . this doesn't even have anything to do with Black people! It's got to do with the left! They want to have conversations about cultural appropriation, yet when it comes to the Jews . . . okay, I need to calm down, regroup, and come back with a better argument.

I know that if I keep arguing, it'll just cement her view that I've gone crazy, so I bite my tongue and move on. Instead I tell her about the paranormal jar of saffron taking up its own shelf.

'How big is the jar of saffron?' she says, more interested in its dimensions than the paranormal activity.

'Like the biggest jar of pickles you've seen in the supermarket, times two.'

'Is it powder or threads?'

'It's not powder, it's the worms. Threads.'

'Red threads?'

'Yes.'

'That's the valuable one. You know it's the most expensive spice in the world? It's like ten grand a kilo.' Antoinette giggles. 'How much are you worth, Saffron?'

Was that a dig at my weight? Listen, you can tell me to lose weight, or you can throw an Egg McMuffin over the gate of the mansion I'm squatting in, but you can't do both.

'Ideally seven-hundred grand, but I might be worth a bit more at the moment.'

Is Antoinette planting in my mind that I should nick Kanye's red gold, the jar of saffron? And, what, sell it I don't know where? Does LA have a Little India? I can't ask Antoinette those questions without accusing her of encouraging me to steal, so I leave it for the moment.

The fuzz keeps overwhelming our conversation. We knew our mobile phones were out of range in this part of Calabasas, but now it's apparent our walkie-talkies can't be trusted either. She tells me that if our walkie-talkies fail she'll write anything urgent on an Egg McMuffin wrapper and toss the burger over the fence.

'Over.'

'Over.'

'Over.'

Even though I'd fumbled the argument that Black Americans have stolen from Jews, Antoinette's comment about Kanye's ancestors possibly singing in the cotton fields brought something into focus. Here was Kanye, ancestors in chains, and here was me, ancestors in concentration camps.

I breathe out and take in my surroundings. White silk lies everywhere. I realise that, at some point during my conversation with Antoinette, I have lain down on Kanye's bed. Directly under the note '*NO NAPS OR LAYING ON MY BED!!!*'

WRITER'S RETREAT BEGINS

Back in the big blue room, what am I to make of all this? Kanye doesn't appear to be in this mansion, and he certainly wasn't over in the two-storey house. Does that mean he's not anywhere on the property?

I'm travelling through a loop of reverse psychology. I catch the feeling Kanye's not here, then that feeling becomes so strong that I fear I'm dropping my guard and he *is* here, hidden away somewhere on this expansive property. I must shut down the parts of my mind that will push me off the deep end.

I'm torn. This house is freaking me out. But how can I complain? When you're a writer, bad things are good things. Bad things bequeath tales that good things never can. I'm here for the same reason Nine Inch Nails came to California and commandeered the Manson house. Houses hold spirits and stories. *If these walls could talk* . . . The walls have talked already, with their Bible passage.

Don't lose your nerve. Bad for me, good for the book.

WRITER'S RETREAT BEGINS

I set up my workstation in the big blue room, turning the desk to face the frosted glass windows so I can have at least a little bit of warning if whoever rumpled those silk sheets returns.

Chin up. What a gift this property is – it's a writer's residency. Back in Australia, over the years, I have applied for artist residencies – filled out endless paperwork – and not been awarded a single one. Not that I'm bitter.

I fold open my laptop, a notepad and pens to the right, Egg McMuffin to the left.

I decide to start by typing up my encounter with Gavin McInnes. That's fresh in my head. That all happened only five days ago.

DISSECTING A FROG

With the gait of Scott of the Antarctic, I made my way through a New York hailstorm. I was on my way to the warehouse of Catholic broadcaster and right-wing provocateur Gavin McInnes. Like other political firebrands I'd met over my working life, Gavin had his idiosyncrasies when it came to deciding who was in and who was out. He was not a fan of transgender people, feminists or Muslims, but said he loved the Jews. So much so that he met up with Kanye and tried to talk him out of promoting Hitler.

Gavin asked that I not reveal the location of the warehouse where he recorded his talk show, fearing reprisals from his enemies. And perusing his résumé, you soon understood he wasn't being a drama queen. In 2016, Gavin founded the Proud Boys, a fraternity and street gang. Two years later, following a brawl with left-wing protesters in New York City, in which seven Proud Boys were arrested, Gavin relinquished his leadership and left the group. He explained at the time, 'I am told by my legal team and law enforcement that this gesture could help alleviate their sentencing.' An Afro-Cuban American, Errio Tarrio, took over Gavin's role. Later, Tarrio was sentenced to twenty-two years' prison for his involvement in the January 6 attack on the Capitol.

A small open-air car park was attached to Gavin's warehouse. A metal sign screwed to the wall indicated the prime parking spot was reserved for Robert Mugabe, the long-dead Zimbabwean dictator. This was Gavin's type of humour, so I knew the black Jaguar XJR parked in that spot was his.

This was also my type of humour. Without thinking, I was laughing, my wide-open mouth tasting the sleet that was in the air. So, what was the joke? Gavin was announcing he was the boss of this media enterprise by comparing himself to a tyrant. And you're not meant to do that. If you're the boss, you're meant to present yourself as 'one of the guys', obscuring the power you wield over your workers. Gavin doing what you're not supposed to do had elicited a laugh from me.

But surely only a boss who *wasn't* a tyrant would joke about being a tyrant. In which case, comparing himself to Mugabe was self-deprecation, employing irony to convey that he wasn't one. On the other hand, maybe his play was this: 'I'm such an entitled jerk, unlike other tyrants who try to hide it, I'll freely tell you that I am one.' In this scenario, the Mugabe reference is still intentionally ironic, but in the service of tyranny, not self-deprecation.

They say that explaining a joke is like dissecting a frog – you can do it, but the frog dies. Well, the frog is dead. But I have killed it to get to this: if I was fine with Gavin's provocation about Zimbabwean dictator – and ethnic cleanser – Robert Mugabe, where did I get off having a problem with Kanye West's provocation: 'I do love Hitler.'

Woah, woah, woah. Where did I say I had a problem with Kanye's provocation? I mean, I did as a political statement. But what if Kanye was playing with fire *as an artist*? Did I have a problem with that? Spotting this Mugabe sign had popped that question into my head, so that is what I ended up trying to square in my interview with Gavin McInnes.

The studio was as white as the hailstorm I had just walked in from, a single square of greenscreen at the far end. Behind a desk, Gavin was wrapping up a segment for his show *Get Off My Lawn*. His producer, in a booth to one side, tapped away at buttons and took Gavin's sarcastic abuse.

When he was done, Gavin approached me, gesturing to two leather chairs in one corner of the studio that wouldn't have been out of place in a hunter's den. A camera mounted on a tripod pointed to these furnishings. It was not just a place to sit, it was a set.

'If we did it here, we could do both at once,' he said. He wanted to interview me while I interviewed him.

I had feared this. That he had asked to meet here in order to put me on his show.

'I just feel like – you must know – that it's sort of like ... things just get ... things just get explosive, you know what I mean?'

I was incoherent, weaselling around what I wanted to say. But he still knew what I meant.

'Oh, you're worried about being cancelled if you're seen with me?'

While Gavin, a red-bearded Scottish-Canadian American, described himself as right wing, others preferred the term 'fascist'.

'You feel appearing with me would be endorsing my views somehow.'

Gavin looked miffed, disappointed by my wimpy attitude. We headed to the bar across the room, which was used as a set too.

'What do I need to know about Jewish people and Black people in America?' I said, straightening myself on the bar stool.

'Well, much to Jews' chagrin, they're not friends. American Jews have wanted to unite with Blacks since before Martin Luther King was assassinated. And I don't know why. Blacks don't like Jews. They actually fear them.'

He said he knew this from his conversations at the gym.

'So, if you talk to a poor Black person – we say "working class", but a lot of them don't work – at my boxing gym, their attitude is – it's not even animosity, it's just fear. I think they see Jews as the ultimate whites. And if you fuck with them, you vanish, you'll die. You'll just disappear. It's almost like fucking with a British colonialist in India. Pre-revolution, pre-independence, you're just brown trash. You'll die.'

Gavin said he defended Jews to the Black people at the gym.

'Now, I think it's retarded that they don't like Jews, but it's not going to change anytime soon. And they have this myopic obsession. Like, rappers, they think that all these Jews are getting rich off them. And I'm like, dude, you'd be nowhere without these Jews monetising your stupid poetry. You're just really a karaoke poet, is what rap is. And you got monetised by Jews. They made you rich with one or two hits. You're good for life.'

He wrapped up his thesis.

'Jews are high-IQ whites who don't drink much and end up

accomplishing more than other whites. That's what it comes down to.'

He said it wasn't just the rap industry but a raft of fields where Jews, due to their allegedly high IQ, called the shots. It was getting confusing for me. He agreed with Kanye that Jews controlled the levers of power, but, unlike Kanye, he thought that was a good thing.

So, if I was acting purely out of self-interest as a Jew, should I challenge his overblown claims of Jewish power? Or should I take what I can get? Yes, there is a Jewish octopus sitting atop the globe, its tentacles reaching into the banks, the media and the government, *but in a good way.*

Gavin's enemies called him a white supremacist. To hear Gavin tell it, there were lumps in this argument. His wife is Native American, his producer is Asian-American, his Proud Boy comrade who took over the group's leadership is Afro-Cuban American. To square this circle, the academic left said that some non-white people, or whole communities, had 'become white'. Basically, they sold out in order to reap the rewards of the white system. To these academics 'white' was an insult.

Interestingly, I was learning that Gavin agreed with these academics' analysis that people 'become white'. Although he was glass-half-full about it. To him, 'white' was a compliment.

'I consider Jews white. I consider a lot of people white. Puerto Ricans. We talk about America like there's all these different groups. But they're all basically white except *maybe* lower-middle-class and down Blacks. They have different accents, totally different culture, different experience. And I don't mind hearing about racism from that group. But when you hear about it from the guy who plays

Mandalorian on *Star Wars*, Pedro Whatshisname from Chile, it's like, "Dude, you have a Conquistador's name. You speak a European language. Shut the fuck up."'

He said Black people were often white too. For him, 1968 was the dividing point. If you were Black before then, you were Black, but if you were Black and born after 1968, you might as well be white.

'Martin Luther King got assassinated in '68, and everyone went, "Oh my fucking God, what is going on?"'

He meant white people were slapped in the face; that single bullet was a crescendo. They could no longer deny Black people in America had suffered under racism.

'From that moment forward, we have been bending over backwards to keep Blacks happy. That's why if you're born after 1968, 1970 – I'm not listening to you talk about racism. You can go fuck yourself. If you're seventy-five years old, like, a guy who's at my local, I'll sit down and I'll listen to him. He can spout off. He was around when it was a thing. But not after 1970. We kissed their ass all through the seventies.'

He said the seventies was the transition decade, when Black people gained cultural standing and a degree of political power. 'Black Power, afros. Black Panthers stormed the Capitol – with guns! They stormed the Capitol armed, and we were like, "Cool!" And funk is cool, and disco, and rap, and everything.'

Gavin said utopia had been attained.

'By the eighties, we were all done. There was no more racism. Everything was cool. Everyone told racist jokes to each other, the way you would to your friends at the firehouse, or at the boxing gym, or at the pub.'

Racism was over, he felt, so you could ironically goof about racism.

'It was done. The whole of America was like Pittsburgh, which is still pretty non-racist to this day. It's a very working-class town.'

Rolling into the nineties, Gavin brought himself into this history of race in America.

'And then political correctness started creeping up in the nineties. It was still on the outskirts, but it was gaining traction. Blue-haired women who dreamed of a world without men and said white people were evil. I think I personally held back the political correctness movement for the entire Western world, like Sisyphus. I started *Vice* magazine. We held it back. It was the most influential young person's magazine. It dominated the college mentality.'

This morning, I had considered the ironic parking sign from all angles. But in the nineties, *Vice*'s ironic humour was simply taken as progressive. The logic being, Christians and conservatives were uptight, so mucking around – which included trying to ensure progressives didn't become histrionic like conservatives – was considered progressive.

As such, *Vice* was peppered with Hitler references, dealing with him in a free-wheeling way. From a fashion section, 2004:

> Nail Art: Great Military Monsters. Our old buddy Georgia thought it would be funny to paint the five military leaders she admires the most (in terms of battlefield tactics, not social philosophy) onto her nails, so she did it and sent them to us. Hitler's the best. The best nail that is.

Was Kanye's flirtation with Nazism actually Nazism? Or was it more a creative impulse, like painting Hitler on your nails because you thought it would be funny?

'When the tsunami of political correctness was trying to get through, *Vice* was holding it back,' Gavin continued. 'And then around 2005, my arms started to shake. I was losing it.'

Gavin marked 2008, the year of a US Presidential election, as the year his arms buckled. 'We got Obama.' All was lost.

To Gavin, not only was President Barack Obama white, he was the worst type: a blue-haired white woman.

'Obama said it's 1965 again. Everything is racist. Everyone is racist. And he said that because that's how these fucking fat bitches are. And that's what he is. He's a fat female communist. He's his mother, his white mother. He's not Black. He can't play basketball. He's like Kamala Harris.'

Harris was born to a Tamil Indian mother and Jamaican father.

'Kamala Harris, Obama – they're wiggers.' Gavin explained the meaning of that term, popular in the nineties. 'They're white people pretending to be black. And those kinds of people tend to be really anti-white.'

He turned to the man of the hour.

'And then there's people like Kanye, where they can go from black to white. Kanye's basically a white dude.'

WHITE ON WHITE CRIME

I stop typing. I tear another bite out of the Egg McMuffin and chew over Gavin's theory. Which is that black people who don't like white people are self-hating white people. I was familiar with the notion of white people trying to be Black, and the notion of Black people trying to be white. But here, according to Gavin, were Black people trying to be white trying to be Black. That's quite the bureaucracy.

It strikes me again. Gavin's theory on race matches that of his ideological enemy, the social-justice warrior on campus, the blue-haired white woman. She, too, believes that race is a social construct. That there are no meaningful distinctions between humans in a biological sense; rather, society imposes those distinctions upon us. Like Gavin, she would believe his Native American wife and his Asian-American producer are only different 'races' in so much as we decide they are.

But I'm more interested in how I can make this theory on race work for me. I screw up the Egg McMuffin wrapper. Something has been weighing on my mind since yesterday, when I was readying myself to cross the stream and Antoinette shouted down from the bank, 'This is like a cancellable kind of thing. Breaking into a Black man's house. I mean, you can do it, you're Jewish. But what have I got? Greek?'

She meant that in the industry we both work in, the arts, you can't be seen to be a white person screwing over a Black person. And moving into a Black man's home without his permission could be seen as exactly that. But, she inferred, my Jewishness alleviated this problem – my minority status makes me *not quite* white, in that foggy way that identity works. So, punching the numbers into the identity politics calculator, it was okay for me to move in to Kanye's house.

But was it?

Gavin couldn't have made it clearer. Black Americans see Jews as not only white but 'the ultimate whites'.

So my enemies could point to my squatting as an infraction of the rule that a white person can't be seen to screw over a Black person.

But not so fast. Gavin also claimed that Kanye has 'become white'. So if he's hiding out somewhere on this enormous property, and we confront each other, it will be a face-off between two people who couldn't be whiter.

THE THIN WHITE DUKE

Gavin met Kanye in a different warehouse, a 'secured location', in late 2022. Although Gavin didn't fully see him, because Kanye had donned a black balaclava with no eyeholes.

The meeting was organised by the proudly antisemitic political operative and commentator Nick Fuentes, who was willing to give Gavin a pass for his love of the Jews because he agreed with him on other matters, like the dangers of feminism. Gavin described both himself and Nick as 'anti-femites'.

What did he learn from that catch-up?

'Ye isn't like the people at my gym. He may have grown up poor, and he was definitely a legit Black dude, but he's been an elite for so long that I think you've got to think of Ye today as David Bowie. And David Bowie did say Hitler was awesome.'

It's true. In 1976, the glam rocker described himself as an 'Aryan superman', saying, 'Adolf Hitler was one of the first rock stars.' And that same year he was detained at the Polish–Russian border for possessing Nazi memorabilia. Small world. My grandparents crossed that same border while fleeing the Nazis.

Later in his career, Bowie explained this fascination with Nazism as being 'theatrical', with drug-induced depression and paranoia egging him on.

'Bowie was saying shit like that because, as an artist, you want to always be saying the most outlandish, never before thought of things,' says Gavin.

Along with sharing Bowie's artistic impulse, does Kanye share his depression and paranoia?

Even with a balaclava hiding his face, Gavin said he could read he was a broken man.

'With Ye, I don't think he's seeing his kids much. And he said to me, "I don't give a shit about myself. Why would I care about Jews?"'

Gavin sighed and locked his eyes on mine. 'I tried to talk him off the ledge, as far as Nazi stuff goes.' The main argument he laid out to Kanye: the Jews he hated – the Hollywood lawyers and music executives – weren't really Jews, in the same way Barack Obama wasn't really a Black person. Rather, these 'Jews' were – you guessed it – blue-haired white women.

Kanye was not receptive to Gavin's advocacy for the Jewish people.

'I don't even know how much he likes Hitler,' he said. 'Does he mean he likes him like he liked Darth Vader?'

Was Kanye drawn to Hitler like I was drawn to skeletons on heavy-metal album covers back in primary school?

'I think at the end of the day it's art,' Gavin finally concluded. 'And he's brought art from music to fashion, and now it's in politics.'

This tangled the matter even further. If I was cool with artists employing Nazi allusions in order to provoke, but not with politicians doing the same thing, what happens when an artist decides to become a politician? Kanye promoted political figures like Donald Trump, and had said he'd run for president himself.

Returning to the scene of the frog that I killed by dissecting it – there was the possibility that Kanye was faking being political for artistic ends. More knots in knots in knots.

'Those of us in the political realm are used to very definitive answers,' Gavin said. '"I like Hitler." It seems kind of cool. In the art world, that's an interesting thing to say. In the political sphere, it's downright confusing at best.'

THE SHATTERED GLASS

In one of the silver fridges in the blue mansion's industrial kitchen, fourteen bottles of sake are stacked sideways. I help myself to one. I am not one of those Jews who don't drink much, whom Gavin commends.

When was the last time someone prepared food in this place? What looks to be algae is floating in a bottle of cooking oil, which suggests this place is long abandoned, but an apple in the refrigerator is yet to shrivel. What the heck do I know about fruit and thermodynamics?

There is no grandfather clock. In lieu of that, every hour or so, a vibrating hum erupts from behind one of the walls. The best I can figure, this has something to do with electricity, keeping the kitchen appliances alive and well.

I twist the knob, turning on one of the silver ovens. Why did I only bring one pair of socks? They got soaked hiking through the woods. I open the oven door and lay them out on the rack.

This lifehack of drying my socks in the oven struck me five minutes ago. I've been walking around all day in bare feet.

I head to the patio from where I entered the mansion last night, a glass in one hand, a bottle of sake in the other. The rain is pattering down. I'm happy to read on the label that this drop is 17 per cent alcohol, more than three times that of beer.

Swigging my sake, I gaze at the light-fitting on the patio. The one designed to look like a Victorian-era gas streetlamp.

What?

The panes of amber glass that make up the lampshade are cracked, veins running everywhere. In fact, one of these plates of glass lies smashed on the ground. I remember staring at this lampshade last night, before discovering the sliding doors were unlocked, and the plates of glass were not cracked then.

I see now that one of the doors has cracked too, a spider's web spreading through the glass. That absolutely wasn't there last night.

A thunderous creak and splosh come from inside the house.

Running through the sliding doors, up the blue hallway, down the white wormhole, reaching the big blue room, I look up to the ceiling. One of the eighteen plastic sheets in the skylights has succumbed to the build-up of rainwater, leaves and debris. Frustratingly, it's the skylight right above the desk. I dart to retrieve my soaked laptop and wipe it across my jumper.

People are always telling me to 'read the room'. Okay, I will. The other skylights are being pushed to their limits, stretching, distending. This room couldn't make it clearer: it doesn't want me here. The house is telling me to stop typing – to shut up. I'll sleep somewhere else tonight.

KANYE'S BED

I stretch myself out, as if on a medieval torture device. There is still plenty of mattress before my hands could reach the bedhead or my feet could reach the end of the bed.

I pull myself up, kneel on the pillows and peek out the window. From up here, one floor up from the room full of ragdoll Holocaust monkeys, I can take in the street and the front grounds. These are more prudent sleeping quarters than the big blue room. I'll be able to spot a car approaching or a person lurking about – Kanye or otherwise.

I left my drinking glass back at the mansion, but remembered to bring the bottle of sake. I take another swig. I reckon this is loosening me up, emboldening me to spend the night here. And I need to be emboldened because strike what I said just before: this is *more dangerous* than the big blue room. My fingertips brush the note taped to the bedhead: *'NO NAPS OR LAYING ON MY BED!!!'*

Gavin's spin was that Kanye's praise for Hitler might be art, not Nazism. But I've been pondering that. Kanye took a billion-dollar hit to his personal wealth, losing his Adidas deal, rather than smooth things over with the Jews. That doesn't sound like art, that sounds like a man who has a deep-rooted beef with the Jews. And what would a man like that do if he found a Jew in his bed?

(Kanye will later defend himself against claims he hates Jews. On the track 'Vultures', he makes this case: 'How am I antisemitic? I just fucked a Jewish bitch.')

I sink back into the bed, my eyelids heavy. I'm trying to remember the bare bones of the Goldilocks fairytale.

So she climbs through the window of a stranger's home. And she tries out the different beds.

The floor in the blue mansion is too hard. But this bed in the two-storey house is juuust right.

Oh, but there's porridge too. That happens before she tests the beds, if I recall correctly.

The open bottle of sake by the bed is too stale. But this one from the fridge is juuust right.

And then the three bears return home. What happens when the bears come home and find Goldilocks asleep in their bed? As the blond-haired guy in the bed, that seems important. But that's the bit I can't remember. Does Goldilocks get eaten up? Or is that Little Red Riding Hood?

I'm drifting off to the land of nod. As I cross the threshold, from this world into dreamland, I'm picturing a pair of socks, but I don't know why.

THE NEXT BLOODY MORNING

I wake up to blood on the sheets. I flinch and pull myself up, sitting upright on the bed. A red streak arcs across the sheet. I scan the room, even though I don't know what I'm looking for. Something from the woods? Springing up, now standing atop the bed, I shake out the quilt. Casting my eyes down, I spot smudges of blood where I've just placed my feet.

Sitting on the side of the bed, I pull my foot up and examine the sole. Shards of amber glass, which I immediately recognise from the shattered Victorian-style lamp on the patio, are embedded in my foot.

I know if I tell Antoinette that this strikes me as odd, she'll brush it off the same way she brushed off my story of the jar of saffron. *Your feet were cold and numb when you ran from the patio to discover the burst skylight. That's why you felt nothing, stepping onto the shards.*

But how would she explain the spider-web crack in the sliding door that absolutely wasn't there the night before? And why, out of eighteen skylights, was it the one above my writing desk that burst open? This is the house telling me I don't belong here.

I pluck out the shards of glass. My shoes are still damp from the night I arrived, so I head outside, limping barefoot to take my morning toilet break. I make my way into the woods behind the mansion, spotting the little shovel that I stabbed into the earth yesterday.

The sky is threatening to break open. The dirt is the worst of both worlds. Muddy enough that my hands and feet become filthy – and then anything I touch, my hair, my clothes – but not muddy enough to soften the earth, which would make digging this hole less arduous. I'm on my knees, encircled by leaves and purple flowers, spearing the earth again and again, levering up small bundles of dirt. By the time the hole is deep enough, mud and sweat are dripping from my stubble.

SQUAT

I pull down my pants. I squat at Kanye's. I remember that man, the one who crouched outside our hotel in downtown LA and opened his bowels. Now I'm glad I didn't act high and mighty – *What kind of lowlife would defecate where one shouldn't!* – when I wrote about him.

Usually I wouldn't include my toilet breaks in a book, but I'm trying to stay true to the artistic spirit of things. Driven by creative impulses, I feel I must. Because when Kanye West's pastor told me stories, *he* kept in the parts where people defecated. It was a big theme, actually.

SHIT

Based purely on the surroundings of the Cornerstone Christian Church, it would be hard to make a call whether the area was rich, poor or somewhere in between. Down the road, hundreds of Amazon delivery trucks were parked in a lot. Heading the other way, strip malls with Starbucks and KFC. Across the road from the church, a park was hosting a fun fair.

This neighbourhood sat next to Calabasas, one of the wealthiest cities in America, so while it was a step down, it was still another of America's wealthiest locales.

'Northridge is where people who can't afford to live in Calabasas buy houses,' a friend of Antoinette's had told me the night before. 'It's kind of a nice suburban area. It's where the '94 earthquake hit the hardest.' (She had attended school in Calabasas and said the kids would call it Cala*blackless*.)

You might expect that Kanye, a brash LA celebrity, attends some kind of megachurch, but this was not that at all. Antoinette and

I pulled into a small car park, cordoned off by a literal white picket fence. There was no giant LCD screen announcing the service times. Rather, in the modest front garden, a sign the size of an Adidas shoebox read: 'Please Do Not Pick The Roses.' The church was long and low, ranch-style, with a white facade.

A very broad arch led inside the building, where the ranch style continued. Thick wooden beams crossed the ceiling and cut grey rocks outlined the raised stage.

When we arrived, Pastor Ron Nagin was already preaching from the pulpit. Antoinette and I easily found seats; there was room for two hundred, but the church was only half full. Like Cala*blackless*, only pink faces could be found here in this Northridge house of worship, including that of Pastor Ron.

'Sometimes we get an obscure view of who Jesus is,' he was saying. 'Our Saviour was born roughly two thousand years ago. He was born in a dumpy, obscure, hick town. One of those places where everyone watches UFC. They have a shotgun on the back of their pick-up truck. And if they shot it and grilled it, that was dinner. That was the kind of town that our Saviour grew up in.'

I was already loving this sermon.

'And so, contrary to popular opinion, Jesus was not this long-haired, effeminate-looking guy. He didn't have long hair with product in it. And sometimes, when you see the picture of Jesus with the product in his hair, with nails and a flowing gown, you wouldn't get the impression that this is someone that you want to live for. Most certainly not someone you'd want to die for. You can't worship someone that you think you could take, right?'

Congregants murmured in agreement.

Pastor Ron's own hair was curly. He had the energy of what, in the seventies, would have been considered 'a real man'; he didn't have a bushy moustache, but looked like the type of man who would.

'The real Jesus wasn't like that. He had short hair. He was a construction worker – calluses on his hands, big biceps from swinging a hammer, good shape. He is UFC Jesus. Sword. Eyes like blazing fire. Coming in on a white stallion. Ready to come and open up a can of whoop-butt.'

Not only did Pastor Ron not go with 'whoop-*ass*', the usual wording in this expression, but he softened his voice when said 'butt'. I felt like UFC Jesus wouldn't have pulled his punches like that.

Pastor Ron said too many preachers made Jesus a sissy. And in so doing they'd pussified the symbol of the faith, the cross, too. It wasn't a beautiful glistening charm, like the one dangling from the necklaces of Christians around the world.

'"Excruciating" literally means "from the cross", because the pain and the shame of the cross was so altogether horrifying that a word had to be created for it. [Fact check: true.] What we know from those who have studied it from a biological perspective is that crucifixion is a slow painful death by asphyxiation. Lungs would cease to fill with air after a man was beaten, just profusely, with a cat-o'-nine-tails.'

He said the clean design of the cross found on jewellery – two planks intersecting at right angles – obscured the actual design of these devices.

'To cause the man who's being crucified to endure more torture, for a greater period of time, they would erect a little seat underneath his bottom. To keep him up, so that he would not slouch down and die too quickly.'

Pastor Ron appeared in pain himself as he spoke, his face contorting, its pinkness turning purple.

'Men were known to get off the seat, to kind of commit suicide – to hasten death. And so, what they would do is they would drive a nail through the penis of the man, to hold him onto that seat so that he would suffer, suffer, suffer, suffer, as long as he possibly could. Brutal, absolutely brutal. This was done publicly. This was not done in obscurity. This was done in public centres. This would be done today in front of a supermarket like Northridge Mall.'

We were in a house of God, the holiest of holies, but Pastor Ron was nothing if not an honest storyteller.

'And it was known that, at this moment, one would become so filled with pain that they would become incontinent – including Jesus! – and they would literally just crap all over themselves, onto the cross, and they would bleed and sweat. And at the bottom of the cross would be the sweat, the blood and the faeces.

'In this condition, a man had been so stripped of his masculinity, so stripped of his dignity, so stripped of his honour, that the person being crucified had no way to retaliate except to curse the people below. And they would try to urinate on the people who were mocking him, so horrible was the crucifixion.'

By Pastor Ron's telling, too many preachers decided all this was too offensive and went with the goody two-shoes version of the faith. Not him.

'The cross *is* offensive. The cross is shameful. It is disgusting. And the cross is where Jesus went. And it should trouble us, and it should horrify us, and it should assault us, and it should offend us. One of the largest churches in America – the pastor says, "We don't talk about sin. We don't talk about blood. We don't talk about death. We don't talk about hell. We don't talk about the cross, because we don't want to talk about anything that would be offensive." Well, then you don't talk about Jesus.'

And that's why I told you about squatting over the hole in the woods behind Kanye's mansion. Pastor Ron insists that any story is incomplete without every detail, no matter how repulsive.

Jesus shat on the cross.

THE TRUMPET

Pastor Ron had wrapped up the service but was being cornered by congregants, so Antoinette and I went wandering.

We came across a man called Mark, in his sixties, who called the church car park home, sleeping in his jalopy there most nights. He was currently relaxing on a bench in the front garden, near where the sign instructed people to please not pick the roses.

'So are you here for a shower?' he asked, as I approached. He oversaw the shower program at the church, for people who slept rough. I made a mental note that I needed a shave.

A long, wild beard, which seemed to have exploded in several directions, sprouted from Mark's face. He was twitching a key in his big hand, the tag reading 'Cornerstone Christian Church'.

'That's why you have the key, so you can open up for the showers?' I tried as small talk.

'No, I have the key because Kanye West said I'd be his campaign manager to run for president.'

Mark spoke in a tone that could be taken as droll. So there were two options for what he meant by this: he was an eccentric fellow who held this delusion in his head or he was being sarcastic.

'Kanye's listening to me. He's got a megaphone. So if he's saying what I'm saying, everyone's going to know it.'

As he continued, it dawned on me that there was a third option. And, amazingly, this turned out to be the one that was true: Kanye West *had* enlisted him as his campaign manager.

Four months earlier, Kanye had been seeking a new location for Donda Academy once again. The mother of one of the students lived opposite this church and noticed a realtor's sign out front – a bunch of empty classrooms were available for lease. So Kanye popped by the church to discuss his plans.

'Kanye was having a meeting with Pastor Ron at the time that this church normally has its prayer meeting,' Mark said. 'So I walked in thinking I was going to a prayer meeting. I said, "Oh, you're Kanye West. Ron told me you were interested in the place. Boy, am I glad you're here." I guess he instantly liked me. I made a good first impression on him. "Can I have a job at your school?" That was my opening line.'

Mark told Kanye that God had conferred upon this church a political calling. Way back in the nineties, it was aligned with the Christian Coalition of America, a Republican-leaning organisation. According to Mark, Pastor Ron had dropped the ball, and this church needed to steer back to its political mission.

'For about an hour with this little group, which was a round-table discussion, I was able to speak about a third of the time. And Kanye was liking what I was saying. So he asked me for my phone number.'

The two of them must have really gelled for Kanye to act that quickly.

'And the following Monday, he called. "I want you to be my campaign manager to run for president." So he invites me down to his factory in Crenshaw, South Los Angeles. And Nick Fuentes is there.'

Nick was the proud despiser of Jews – the political operative, the white nationalist – who had arranged the meeting between Gavin McInnes and Kanye.

'And they're plotting to take down Trump. And I'm saying, no, you don't want to do this, because Reagan said his Eleventh Commandment was "Don't speak evil of your fellow Republicans." I said, you're not going to win the evangelical vote doing it this way.'

I became dizzy taking in the picture: Kanye, one of the world's most famous celebrities; Mark, the elderly man who slept in his car; and Nick, the young white nationalist (part-Mexican, by the way), plotting to take over America at Yeezy headquarters.

Insisting that Kanye shouldn't run for president made Mark's role as campaign manager for his presidential run untenable. But Kanye still dug him, so his role morphed. Kanye now wanted Mark to become his religious instructor.

'He tells his business manager he is going to pay me to do Bible study.'

Picking up that Kanye felt this special connection with Mark, Pastor Ron thought this development could be handy in negotiating Kanye's lease on the church's classrooms.

'Ron gave me six hundred bucks. He wanted the deal to go through, so he decided to help me. He said, "Get some nice clothes, look a little better."'

Pastor Ron also gave him a key to the church – the one we saw him holding when we first started talking.

'So, Kanye comes in. I prepared a Bible study for him in one of the classrooms.'

But Kanye had assumed he'd be learning as part of a group. That Mark had been planning a one-on-one session made him suspicious.

'He says, "Well, I don't do this in silos. And that's very Jewish of you." And I'm thinking – is that an insult?'

Neither Mark nor I could figure out why one-on-one instruction would be perceived as Jewish.

Over the following weeks, Kanye turned up to a few more Bible classes, then just stopped rocking up.

At the start of Year Seven, I asked my parents for a trumpet and they bought me one. I turned up to trumpet class a few times, and then just stopped. In hindsight, I can see what a spoilt, selfish, entitled jerk I was. So I have to imagine some of these same human foibles played into Kanye's impulsive behaviour – hiring a guy to be his religious instructor, presumably a pretty weighty and significant commitment, and then just dropping him without a word.

Tamar had told me Kanye was taking weekly Torah classes. Was that happening at the same time as he was under Mark's tutelage? Or did one follow the other? Regardless, Kanye was clearly a man searching for something. And he thought he might find it in ancient scripture.

Mark said that he'd seen Kanye only a few days ago, pulling up into this very church car park.

THE TRUMPET

'I said, "Long time no see." And I said, "I can't call you." I guess he threw out his phone or something.'

Kanye didn't give Mark his new number. Kanye had finished with this trumpet.

KANYE'S PASTOR

Pastor Ron had metal rods in his back, which made it painful for him to even sit. Sitting across from Antoinette and me near the front of the church, he looked more tormented than crucified Christ in the painting on the wall nearby.

During the service, the Eucharist had been offered. When Antoinette had reached the front of the queue, she took the wafer and wine, then requested Pastor Ron pray for her rabbit. Now that we were all together, he was asking her more about the pet.

'She's up and down, Seaweed. She's dying one day and okay the next. She has cheated death four or five times.'

The pastor, who I would discover had cheated death several times himself, was about to hit his seventieth birthday. He explained that he saw Kanye's leasing of the classrooms as an inflection point. It was time to pull the trigger on several things: things he'd been meaning to do for a while. He was going to retire, sell his house and move to Arizona. In fact, this morning was his final service as pastor. A Hispanic congregation was taking over here at Cornerstone.

'Is it true the new congregation is trying to kick Mark out of the car park?' I asked. (Mark had told me this.)

'Really, to be fair,' said Pastor Ron, 'Mark would sleep in the church and pee his pants and pee on the chairs.'

As with his sermon on the crucifixion, bodily waste was part of the story, and he wasn't going to leave it out. He empathised with the Hispanic pastor trying to run Mark out of the car park.

'He's destroyed five chairs in the church. I mean, I've been so nice to Mark. I've brought him over, cooked him steak dinners – rib-eye steaks and stuff. And it's just too gross to tell you. He's a slob. And I said, "Mark, you're ruining our chairs. Put down plastic or sit on a towel or something."'

Wanting to steer away from this discussion of bodily functions, I asked about Kanye's involvement in the church, but that didn't work.

'I went into church a couple of months ago,' he said. 'Ye was there. And Mark was sitting next to him. The smell of urine – oh my God. How could you go sit next to someone as famous as Ye, and you've peed in your pants? Come on, man. And you leave your urine bottle up on a counter where people serve food.'

Pastor Ron drifted further away from the subject of Kanye, and even more into the scatological.

'And look, I have a heart for that tall guy you saw in the church today, Lenny. I found him sleeping in front of the church about fifteen years ago. I let him stay in the church for years – until he started pooping in the trash cans and leaving it there.'

Now, I could take the snarky position that the pastor was happy to pontificate from behind the pulpit that human waste was all part of the holiest of holy, the crucifixion, yet when Mark and Lenny do him the favour of shitting and pissing in his church, he complains? But, to be honest, if I ran a church, I too would find it exacerbating. There are toilets on site, Mark and Lenny. Just use them.

When they sat down to negotiate the lease, Pastor Ron had been briefed that Kanye was a celebrity, but he thought, so what? This was LA. Everyone was either a celebrity or claiming to be one.

'He was nice, very cordial. Unfortunately, that day my brother had died – my triplet brother. And so I apologised to Ye if I seemed kind of off. But it was a difficult day. It was a day of contrast.'

His shoulders drooped. He had learnt just how famous Kanye was soon enough.

'The paparazzi got to be a bit much. They were coming into the church, and we had to tell them: you can't be taking pictures during the service. It just got to be obnoxious after a while.'

'We're not paparazzi, we're not like TMZ,' Antoinette threw in. (Later I realised TMZ might have the moral high ground over me. *Hey, we might have taken long-lens photographs of Kanye's mansion, but at least we didn't sleep in his bed and swig down his sake.*)

'I don't understand why a lot of people get so enamoured over famous people,' Pastor Ron went on. 'The only person that I really was excited about meeting was a man named Jim Whitaker. He was the first American to climb Mount Everest.'

This revelation cracked open the mystery of why Pastor Ron's body was in the shape it was in – he had scaled a mountain himself, in his thirties, but fallen off. But that hadn't dissuaded him from continuing a life of extremes. He loved escaping to the desert for days on end, or camping solo in the woods, especially during storms.

'I fly a power paramotor. You know what that is? It's a motor on your back with a propeller. You're hanging from a parachute.'

He pulled up a news clip on his phone, from 2015. A wide shot revealed a person paramotoring over mountain ranges, a police helicopter in hot pursuit. Now it cut to the man after he had landed, the cops handcuffing him. In this close-up we saw that the offender was Pastor Ron. He had inadvertently flown over a prison, and the sheriff's department thought he was dropping in weapons or drugs. He hadn't been, the matter was cleared up, and he was sent on his way.

'I've had thirty-six surgeries. I've had both knees, both hips replaced. I have rods in my back, rods in my neck. They've got to do more surgery on my neck. I'm just very, very active.'

He lived dangerously in his day-to-day life, too. People told him not to lease the classrooms to Kanye, because of his Hitler remarks. He was unperturbed.

'No doubt he has said some controversial things – some that were taken out of context. To me, it's not that relevant, because it's about the kids and not about Ye. It's about what's best for the kids, not the individual who owns the school. I've talked with Ye quite a bit and he's a good man. He has a heart for kids. Look, we all say things that get misunderstood. And you hear all this construction going on? He's doing it for the kids.'

Power tools were squealing like pigs from somewhere outside the church, although my ears had ignored them until it was brought to my attention. Kanye was remodelling the classrooms.

'Is he there now, Kanye?' I asked.

Pastor Ron said he wasn't. But did that mean he really wasn't, or had the pastor just filed me away with TMZ and other paparazzi? Did he think Kanye, his business associate and congregant, needed to be protected from me?

Next the pastor revealed that, just because he wasn't offended by Kanye, that didn't mean he was incapable of being offended.

'We haven't had a Christian school here in decades. We've had secular schools, but they come in this sanctuary, for a parent meeting or whatever, and they cover up our cross with butcher paper. They cover up the Ten Commandments. And it's offensive. So we were glad to have a Christian school come in.'

Antoinette jumped in.

'John, you missed something in the church service, didn't you?'

I had no idea what she was talking about.

'You were too embarrassed to go up and accept . . .' she petered out.

I still wasn't following.

'The baptism,' she mumbled.

Oh, yes. During the service, Pastor Ron had asked if anyone needed a baptism. I hadn't felt I did, so stayed in my seat. Antoinette had then whispered I should approach Pastor Ron after the service and request a private one, then upsell him on the idea that Kanye should be there, to dunk me, or hold the towel.

Sitting before Pastor Ron, I cringed at the thought of trying to make this request sound natural.

'How does that work?' I tried. 'Like, accepting Jesus?'

'You have to come to a point to realise that you are not the ruler of your own life,' Pastor Ron said. 'That there is someone greater who created you. So you either believe that you evolved from an ape and you're just here by chance, or you believe that there is a God.'

'If one does a baptism, can you bring friends?' I asked, easing into the upsell. 'Because I think, because to add to the importance, because I thought, if Kanye —'

Pastor Ron interrupted. 'The reason you're here today is not for Kanye. I believe God brought you here. You want to be baptised? Happy to.'

Not to be a God snob, but in the course of my work I have partaken in vivid and extreme rituals, including an exorcism in Oklahoma, a voodoo ceremony in Haiti and a crucifixion in the Philippines, so a baptism at Kanye's church *without* Kanye felt a bit weak.

I told Pastor Ron I'd left my diary back at the hotel, kicking the can down the road as to when I would be dunked.

'Are you guys a couple?'

'Yes,' I said.

'Oh, are you ever going to propose to this lovely girl? Sorry to put you on the spot.'

Before I could answer, Pastor Ron winced.

'I'm sorry, my neck. I'm in so much pain right now.'

Hey, maybe that was Jesus telling you to mind your own beeswax.

'I have to go into hospital tomorrow, and they're going to decide whether or not they're going to fuse another section of my neck.'

He plucked out his phone again. He wanted to show us a video of his brother, one of the triplets, who had died on the day Kanye first came to the church.

'I didn't have any friends in high school. I didn't date one time. I didn't need anyone. I already had someone exactly like me. And I was incredibly shy. My sister, the other triplet, would bring home friends from school, and I would hide in a cupboard because I didn't want to talk to anyone.'

He kept thumbing away at his phone, trying to find the footage of his brother.

'Me and my brother used to play this game. It's called Shoot Me All You Want. One person would stay on the patio with the BB gun. And you'd have to run from one end of the pool to the other. And if you shouted, "You can shoot me all you want!", the person on the patio could shoot you all they wanted. Right? Until the person ran out the gate.'

Passing the phone to us, I was expecting to see the hijinks of two teenage boys. But, instead, glowing from the screen, were two men in their sixties. This had been filmed only a few years ago. His brother was fleeing through a backyard, past a swimming pool, and Pastor Ron was firing a rifle at him from a patio. Both men were laughing uncontrollably. Pastor Ron stopped shooting and his brother fell to his knees, pulling the widest grin of the happiest man in the world.

'Oh, my goodness, it's really cute,' Antoinette said.

'That is love,' Pastor Ron said. 'Believe it or not, that is love.'

He was now spooling through his phone for something else.

'I'm going to show you a picture, just before he died. This'll break your heart.'

Pastor Ron was right. I didn't know what I was expecting, but it wasn't this. Bent in the foetal position, on the tiles of a bathroom floor, lay an impossibly gaunt man. Another skeleton in this story.

'We couldn't get him off the fentanyl.'

Antoinette and I sat in silence.

'That isn't mud on the bottom of his feet,' Pastor Ron added, true to form. 'That's shit.'

RATTLESNAKES!

I bob down and retrieve an Egg McMuffin (no bacon) from the bridge, no doubt flung over the gate by Antoinette sometime earlier this morning. If she tried reaching me by walkie-talkie, I was probably too deep in the woods, out of range, on my toilet break.

My bare feet are stung cold by the concrete. I wander back to near where I was just squatting and keep going further. Behind the mansion, the woods open out to a grassy, hilly landscape that takes up over 300 acres, running into the Santa Monica mountains. This is where Kanye assembled his prototype beehive domes for the homeless, which the council insisted he dismantle.

The domes are long gone, but I can make out something else in the distance: what looks to be a UFO. Although, instead of shiny metal, cream-coloured wood gently bends around to form the circular structure. It's big, but it sits on its lonesome, with dying grass stretching out near-forever in all directions, so it's also small.

I make my way up the gentle slope. The vessel doesn't seem to be getting closer. What is it? Is Kanye living in there? That would make sense. A new housing prototype and, needing to hide from the world, why not live here?

I finally arrive. The way the boards of weather-worn wood are pieced together, neatly but with every joining line clear, I feel like I'm up close to Noah's Ark.

I slowly begin to circle the UFO.

'Hello?'

Circling further, I reach the entrance. An arch cut into the ark. I poke my head in.

'Hello?'

I don't spot Kanye, or Martians, or Noah.

Rather, pews form a ring around an oak tree growing in the centre, its thick roots octopussing outward. No flooring is laid out here, there's just earth.

A twig of recognition hits me. Yes, I know this. Antoinette waving her phone, showing footage of Kanye's gospel choir singing in worship around that tree. Jesus is King! This UFO served as a church. You could fit maybe a hundred and fifty people in here.

Lying down on a pew, stretching out, I immediately worry the grey clouds above are set to open. There is no roof on this flying saucer ark church; it would be a long and unpleasant sprint back to the mansion if the weather turns.

I unwrap the Egg McMuffin and take a bite. I've brought a bottle of sake to wash it down. What's this? I see Antoinette has penned a message on the greasy wrapper:

RATTLESNAKES!

I immediately know what she means by this. Since we last spoke, Antoinette has read on some website, or in some book, or on a plaque at a nature sanctuary, that rattlesnakes slither through the woods of Calabasas. She already warned me about the mountain lions, black bears, bobcats, coyotes and black widow spiders, but now she has an addition to the danger spreadsheet.

Yet, despite her capital letters and the exclamation mark, my mind doesn't go to what might be lurking in the woods. It goes to a different kind of danger.

THE SHOUT FROM THE DARK

Only one week before I left for America, I hosted a Multicultural Comedy Gala in Newcastle. I dragged four big garbage bags onto the theatre stage and approached the microphone.

'So, Kanye West started praising Adolf Hitler and blaming Jewish people for all the problems in the world,' I began. 'He said Jewish bankers were screwing him over. And he boldly called out these bankers by name on his Instagram.'

Behind me, on a screen, slides flashed up. Headshots of executives from JP Morgan Chase, the largest bank in America.

'So I thought I'd find out more about these Jewish bankers name-checked by Kanye. I hit up their bios on the JP Morgan Chase website. Under Kanye's chief villain, Managing Director Bill Grous, I found this: "Bill is active within the Greek Orthodox community and proudly holds the title of Archon of the Greek Orthodox Church." So Kanye's first Jewish banker was a Greek Orthodox Christian.

'Let's move on to Kanye's next target, the Jewish CEO of the bank, Jamie Dimon. Turns out he's a Greek Orthodox Christian too. In fact, no banker on his list of Jewish bankers is Jewish. And I think there's an important lesson to learn here.'

I paused.

'Greek people are shifty and can't be trusted.'

The crowd liked that one. And it got my point across that Kanye was cherrypicking.

The room was dark, but I could make out a few folks in the front row eyeing the garbage bags surrounding me.

'Adidas decided to cut Kanye loose,' I went on. 'Around that time, I started dating this woman, Antoinette, who was a huge fan of his. The first time I went to her house, she sheepishly took me through her wardrobe, which was filled with thousands of dollars' worth of Yeezy shoes and Kanye fashion.'

I tipped out, one by one, the garbage bags: sneakers, jackets, t-shirts, caps and trackpants.

'She didn't think it was a good look to be wearing this anymore, or even owning it – or even having it known she owned it – lest she be cancelled. She's not Jewish, and she wanted my thoughts on what she should do with all of this.'

That's when an angry shout came from the crowd. 'Give it to the Palestinians!'

I was thrown. Here I was, not in Israel, not discussing Israel. But I continued. 'I needed to come up with something. I thought, all this fabric, why not upcycle it? But I needed a sample. A proof of concept.'

Slides flashed up behind me. In the first one, I was in a garage, the workshop of a costume designer, a friend of Antoinette. The next one showed a pair of Yeezy sneakers on the workbench. They were the colour of a nearly ripe lemon, with blue streaks running through them, giving the effect of a day-glo zebra. The next slide showed the costume designer, elbow in the air, unstitching the panels of one of the sneakers. Next she was stretching these panels over a hat block.

On stage, I reached into my pocket and held up the final product, a Yeezy sneaker reconfigured as a Jewish skullcap, a yarmulke.

'And this is the YEmulke!'

The crowd liked this one too, cheering the Yemulke, which I thrust above my head.

But, walking back to the hotel after the show, my mind wasn't buzzing from the joy of those cheers. My mind had been taken over by the man who had shouted from the darkness, 'Give it to the Palestinians!'

That shout from the dark in the theatre was a pivotal moment for how I thought of the story of Jews in Australia. Or at least a marker of a moment, a premonition. Before that, I hadn't thought of Australia as the type of place where people shout at Jews in public.

Interestingly, the question of Israel is one of the few things Kanye doesn't hold over Jewish people.

'Your thoughts on Palestinians?' a paparazzo once asked him in an airport.

'I don't have enough information on that,' Kanye said. 'I'm straight up from the South Side of Chicago, born in Atlanta. It's love for everybody. But don't pull me to that conversation.

I've got fourteen kids dying every week in my city. So, talk to me about that.'

Whatever Kanye's problem with Jews is, it's something other than Israel.

THE IMP ON THE HILL

I'm pulled out of my thoughts by a dreadful sound. The wind is having its way with the UFO, fighting the joints of the wooden panels, producing squeaks that are almost squeals. The clouds look like they're about to erupt, and I know it's time to head back to the mansion.

Outside the UFO, I gaze down the slope. I can't explain why – childishness? laziness? – but I impulsively lie down on my side, grip the sake bottle to my chest and start rolling down the hill. Gravity does its thing. Over and over I spin, the yellow of the grass and the grey of the clouds blurring into each other. A string of thumpity thumps drumming into my ears. I'm dizzy, but it's too late to stop; this needs to play out. I let out a goofy 'heehee'. This is fun. This is an exorcism of my fears.

Close to the mansion, where the grass ends and the concrete begins, my body decelerates and I come to rest on my back. Motionless, I stare up to the heavens.

The joy of the spin doesn't last. From my viewpoint, I can make out the peak of the hill on the other side of the road. Atop that hill is the wooden lookout deck, belonging to the neighbour who took photos of Kanye's beehive homes and sent them to TMZ. I fumble, pulling my glasses case from my pants pocket, snapping it open, and slipping on my frames. Squinting, this time I'm convinced it's not ambiguous. There's a figure on that lookout deck. I've been spotted.

I leap up and sprint the last little bit to the mansion. I escape up the wormhole to the big blue room, with the Ezekiel scripture chalked on the wall and the bucket accepting the drip that is well past full, a puddle reaching all the way to one of the walls where the mushrooms are joyfully taking over the skirting board.

There's a stench. What's that stench? Demons squeeze through skirting boards and come with a stench.

I run to the industrial kitchen. An oven light is on, but if it wasn't, my nose would still have drawn me here. I pull open the oven door and the full force of the stink hits me. My socks. I put them into the oven yesterday to dry out, then went to sleep in the two-storey house. Now they're a pair of hard, tight balls.

I have to assume there'll be consequences to being spotted by the imp on the hill. I weigh up my options. I could plant myself back in the big blue room. Aurally, I'll be across impending threats; I'll be able to hear the front gate scraping open and, if that happens, duck out the back of the mansion and hide in the woods. But visually, I might as well be wearing Kanye's balaclava with no eyeholes.

The other option is taking shelter in the second storey of the house. Kneeling on Kanye's bloodstained bed and peeking out the window, I will be able to survey the front grounds, the gate, and the street beyond the gate, including the lookout deck on the hill. But I won't be able to hear the front gate scraping open. And, unlike in the mansion, there are no back doors to escape through.

The stench and the dampness in the blue room are too much. The executive chair is soaked, having fallen victim to the rain and debris bursting through the broken skylight. The floor around the chair and desk is drenched, and littered with acorns and muck. The sheets across the other skylights look minutes away from bursting themselves. Kanye's bedroom in the two-storey house it is.

I thread myself back through the wormhole, this time away from the entrance of the mansion. I turn into the hallway and out of the sliding doors whence I entered two nights ago.

Jesus Christ! What is wrong with you, John? I've run over the amber shards of glass on the patio again. And this time I feel it straight away. Damn you, house!

I ease myself to the ground, bend up my foot and pluck out the shards, then get to work on the other foot.

Coming out of the woods two nights ago, making my way down to this patio was easy enough. Climbing back out is more of a struggle, but I get there, albeit my anorak, pants and face are now covered with mud. I might as well be a soldier in camouflage.

I make my way along the back of the mansion, heading for the rear of the garage. A gap divides the two structures and I sprint across it, potentially exposing myself to the imp in the lookout.

This enormous property throws up another surprise. Attached to the back of the garage I discover a whitewashed cottage. The blinds are pulled shut, and the facade is unnervingly normal: a white door with a mail slot, a doorbell and a welcome mat laid out. Normal for a suburban street, but this cottage faces a muddy clearing and the woods beyond. I've no idea if a door inside the cottage gives you access to the garage or if it's a stand-alone structure. I reckon it's intended as lodgings for a gardener or a housekeeper or someone like that.

I've lost my bearings: do I *want* to find someone inside? (Good for the book!) Or am I praying that no one's inside who can call the police, or punch me in the jaw? (If I'm punched in the jaw, is that good for the book?) I guess I can't claim that I'm poking around for Kanye and then chicken out when I find a credible spot he might be hiding.

I approach the door and push the buzzer. The loudness of the *brrrrrng* startles me, piercing through this quiet enclave in Calabasas. Did the imp on the hill hear that?

I'm cringing with both fear and awkwardness. Will someone open the door? I can't see my face, but I can imagine my smile, my lips stretched out, white teeth pushing through a muddy brown visage.

Has it been fifteen seconds or two minutes since I buzzed? Time is losing itself. I press my ear against the door. I can't hear any clomps – footsteps approaching the door. But does that mean no one's home, or that the person inside, hearing the buzz, is holding themselves still as a statue, measuring up what to do?

I pull my head from the door. I've left a muddy ear print.

Another point of no return. I try opening the door.

Unlike the sliding doors on the patio, and the door with the golden doorknob opening to the Holocaust monkeys, this one's locked.

Out of luck, I have to move on. Another gap separates this cottage from the rear of the two-storey house, which means I again could be caught by the long lens of the imp at the lookout.

I drop to the ground and, employing my elbows, worm across the gap.

Parked on the far side of the two-storey house, I find five black military vehicles. I duck behind these, and, deciding to go the shortest distance from A to B, worm my way from one of the enormous tyres to the door of the house. I spring up, turn the golden doorknob and slip inside.

THE BEASTS

Sitting on Kanye's bed, facing the window, I unfold my laptop. I need to keep writing this book, whether the mansion wants me to or not.

One week after meeting Pastor Ron, we returned to Cornerstone church. It was the morning of the Hispanic congregation's first 10 am service, replacing Pastor Ron's. In the back pew, Antoinette and I must have stuck out as gringos; a deacon approached, offering earpieces and receivers. He returned to a mixing desk at the back of the church, leant into a microphone, and began translating the pastor's Spanish sermon.

'When the bird tweets, is he worshipping God?' came the translator in my ear. Then static took over and I did not hear the answer.

With my other ear, I could hear the faint sound of tools screeching and clanging on the other side of the wall. As Pastor Ron had explained to us, Kanye's team were remodelling and building facilities for his school.

THE BEASTS

Antoinette and I skipped out of the service and found Mark, like last week, on the bench in the front garden next to the Please Do Not Pick The Roses sign.

He reckoned he would be pushed out of the car park when Kanye's school opened. He had seen that dynamic play out at other churches.

'They build these classrooms for Sunday school or a day-care centre, because that subsidises their budget. And then the government says homeless people and kids can't be near each other. And that's the end.'

Rather than the cops rolling in, waving batons, these evictions happened in a murkier, bureaucratic way, with low-rung church staff taking care of business.

'They say, "The insurance company says you're not allowed here because you're not insured to be here."'

I tried to imagine Jesus approaching a leper and explaining public liability insurance to him.

Mark hadn't decided where he would go if booted from the car park. He knew that Kanye had ideas for housing the homeless, experimenting with beehive domes.

'They looked like fancy African huts, the ones that I saw. Which doesn't appeal to me.'

He also didn't like Section 8, a government voucher program that's supposed to help low-income people rent houses in the private market.

'I never thought I'd be homeless for ten years. If I had signed up for Section 8 ten years ago, maybe I'd be at the top of the list by now. But these agencies, they have priorities. They're going to help women and children. They're going to help old people, overweight, Black people. There's an order to the way they approach these things. I'm last on the list, as a Christian and a Republican. I have no confidence in the Democrats helping me at all, for all of those reasons.'

Which is why he supported Donald Trump, to the point of sacrificing his job as Kanye's campaign manager. 'We need a rich person with a big mouth that'll speak for the people.'

A cement truck crawled through the car park, disappearing through an open gate. Antoinette and I followed it to the construction site behind the church. Workers, all dressed in black, were pushing wheelbarrows, raising wooden beams and standing around yapping.

We had heard that Kanye insisted those around him wore black, from the parents of the Donda students to the workers on this site. For me, this was art unambiguously going too far. Construction workers wear hi-vis for safety, and Kanye was donning them in black for aesthetics, increasing the danger one would be splattered into a Jackson Pollock.

We drifted over to a green demountable that looked to be the site office.

I knocked and squeaked open the door. Relaxing in a chair with his feet on a desk was a young man who, to my untrained eyes, looked like countless men I passed every day, but who Antoinette later explained was a hypebeast. As far as I could see, he was just decked out in streetwear you could pick up at any mall (this isn't a diss, he looked cool!), but Antoinette understood the subtleties and the codes. His black jacket was Rick Owens, his shoes were Yeezy

Season 1, the shades pushing back his hair Balenciaga. Standing next to him was a woman who, to me, looked like a goth who sits under the clocks at Flinders Street Station, but who struck Antoinette as a 'Glenn Martens–inspired fash girl' in black 'daytime bondage', straps and metal running everywhere.

Neither looked the type to be running a construction site. On the wall, where a site manager would have blueprints of the buildings, were mood boards with magazine cut-outs of tops and shoes.

'Hi,' Antoinette said.

We hadn't prepared a plan for whatever this was we'd just walked into. I was curious as to what Antoinette was going to say next.

'We're not paparazzi.'

This widened the eyes of the Hypebeast. Insisting we weren't paparazzi, before being asked if we were, was like declaring 'I'm not on drugs' apropos of nothing.

'We're just bumbling about,' I said. 'We're bumblers.'

'Bumblers?' the Hypebeast asked.

'I'm a writer,' I said. 'We interviewed Pastor Ron and all that stuff. So there's no particular, like, whatever.'

The Hypebeast was not satisfied with this. 'No particular *what?*'

Before I could get out the word 'agenda', Antoinette chimed in.

'We know the Donda school is opening here, but we're not telling anyone.'

Now his nostrils flared.

'We're just fumbling,' I said, trying to put him at ease.

'We're bubbling,' Antoinette added. We were sounding like Bert and Ernie in a bathtub, about to break into song. His workmate, Daytime Bondage, brushed past me, slipping out the door.

'Is Kanye coming today?' Antoinette asked.

'I don't know about that,' the Hypebeast said.

'Oh, I can see a little *yes* in your eyes,' she giggled. From her perspective, here were two kindred spirits who knew who Rick Owens and Glenn Martens were.

'There's probably someone better you can talk to,' the Hypebeast advised. 'Here, I'll take you out.'

He shepherded us back out through the big gate, into the car park.

'We're not paparazzi, nothing like that.'

'I understand. They're just really big on discretion. Who comes in and out.'

He asked for our names and numbers.

'Just want to connect you with the right person. So the next time that you interact with someone here, it's not less friendly than this.'

He didn't have the accent of a Mafioso, but managed to convey the same vibe.

'What's your name?'

'Antoinette. And yours?'

'Raphael. I just feel like they're going to have a problem if you're back here ... bumbling.'

Out of nowhere, like a moon rising in fast motion, a big bald head slid up before me.

'Maybe this is a better person for you to talk to,' Raphael said.

'Y'all got to leave the property,' said Moonface.

Right away I realised that this man matched the description of the guy who kicked James out of the abandoned Donda schoolhouse in Simi Valley. Bald, heavy-set, white. (Raphael was white too, for those keeping score.)

We backed away.

Antoinette and I regrouped by the Please Do Not Pick The Roses sign. So still on church property, but away from the gate leading to the construction site.

'Kanye's coming today,' Antoinette said.

Her evidence? She pointed to three shiny black Mercedes SUVs in the car park, which hadn't been there fifteen minutes ago. She knew from photos on TMZ that this colour and make of vehicle were Kanye's convoy of choice.

Before I had time to ask more, on the street running along the church garden, another black Mercedes skidded to a halt. Moonface stuck his moon face out the driver's window and pulled a menacing grimace.

We powerwalked to the church building, pushed through the front doors, and took shelter in the foyer. Spanish pleas to Jesus came from the sanctuary. A deacon motioned for us to come in and return to the service. But I felt like exploring. I knew from snooping around the week before that a hallway ran up either side of the sanctuary. On the left were the kitchen, Pastor Ron's office and storage rooms, but the other side led to the classrooms the church was leasing out to the Donda Academy, and they held more interest for me.

We left the foyer and turned down that hallway. A sign screwed to the door of one of the smaller classrooms read 'Math Lab'.

I chuckled, as I had the week before, because, you know, *meth lab*. We arrived at the largest of the classrooms and squished our faces against the window in the door. Last time we'd seen school desks laid out in rows, but now they'd been removed. Instead, in one corner, a tripod, lighting gear and backdrop made up a little photography studio. And it was clear what model had been snapped: hung everywhere were large photos of Bianca Censori, Kanye's new Australian wife. Laid out on the floor were the garments she was modelling in the pictures.

It occurred to me that, if I bumped into Kanye, I needed a line to open with. What was my way in?

Hi, Kanye, I'm from Melbourne, like your wife. Small world.

Hi, Kanye, I'm Jewish, like . . . Jesus!

Hi, Kanye, I'm also a rapper. I won RMIT's Battle of the Bands fronting Raspberry Cordial. Have you heard of them?

Then it struck me that I already had a perfect conversation starter. The Yemulke. The Yeezy sneaker repurposed as a Jewish skullcap. I could just give that to him and the conversation would flow from there.

Except the Yemulke was tucked into my luggage, back at the hotel – a forty-minute drive away. Antoinette and I left the church and jumped in the Jeep.

'Kanye's coming today. There's just no way he isn't,' Antoinette said, convinced by the fleet of black Mercedes, and everyone's skittishness.

In the hotel, taking the lift to our room, we spotted Elvis Costello. He was poised, in a smart suit. I wished I was trying to hunt him down instead of Kanye. Because – mission complete!

But I had nothing hard-hitting to ask him other than if he still performed 'Oliver's Army', the 1979 hit in which the lyrics refer to Catholics in Northern Ireland as white n-words. And I chickened out of asking even that.

In our room, I scooped up the Yemulke, but before we headed out again Antoinette took over as style consultant. It couldn't hurt to try to blend in with the hypebeasts.

Antoinette's wardrobe was largely made up of gender-neutral oversized 'pieces'. She'd been dressing me up in these for months.

'The Kith wolf top,' she said, passing it to me. This was a fluffy brown hoodie with wolves standing against a backdrop of trees.

'Blue jeans or black jeans?' I asked.

'Blue jeans.'

'Nikes or New Balance?'

'New Balance.'

'I shouldn't have given them my real name.' I was thinking about Raphael the hypebeast and Moonface. Now they could google me.

'Don't worry, there are two John Safran writers.'

She was referring to the American author Jonathan Safran Foer.

I said, 'Imagine, on the news tonight: "Jonathan Safran Foer found beaten up on the streets of Los Angeles. A black Mercedes Benz was seen skidding away from the scene."'

Pulling up outside the church, we could see the gate to the construction site was now shut, guarded by Moonface and another bulky man. Antoinette sensed that Kanye must have arrived already.

We drove around the corner and slipped into the foyer of the church. My New Balances squeaked up the hallway. Again I pressed my face against the window of the big classroom door. No Kanye. The room was just as we had left it that morning.

I also pressed my face against the windows in all the other classroom doors, but they, too, were empty, as they had been that morning. Further down the hallway was a door with no window, which had been locked this morning. To be thorough, I twisted the doorhandle, knowing it would still be locked.

Except it wasn't.

I opened the door. Six hypebeasts, twelve eyes, turned to me and Antoinette. They looked us up and down. My fluffy hoodie with the wolves seemed to do the job. They smiled. They thought I was a fellow hypebeast.

'The Yemulke, John,' Antoinette whispered.

I held out the Yemulke and a female hypebeast approached.

'We know Ye's here,' Antoinette said in a friendly tone.

'We just wanted to pass this on,' I said. 'It's a skullcap because, you know, there was a thing between him and the . . .' I petered out, unable to thread the needle of explaining the concept without saying the word 'Jews'.

However, that didn't matter. The hypebeast immediately got it and laughed.

'That's cute.'

This was working. She turned to show her colleagues. On the cusp of all of us hypebeasts having a jolly laugh together, I heard footsteps coming up the hallway.

'You have to go,' boomed Moonface.

THE BEASTS

The smile fell from the face of the female hypebeast. She pushed the Yemulke back in my hands. I might as well have had leprosy, the way she was backing away. For the second time that day Antoinette and I were forced to flee.

QUANDARIES

Stretching out on Kanye's bed, one floor above the Holocaust monkeys, I stop typing.

What is going on at that church? It's mad. Kanye had said he wanted to lease space for his school, but what he had actually done was set up a Yeezy office. Why?

The Yeezy office had previously operated out of a two-storey, 1400-square-metre brutalist building in Calabasas. The monochromatic interior design, including a ten-metre-long sofa, had been showcased in bleeding-edge architectural magazines. They'd been evicted following Kanye's outburst supporting Hitler, but correlation doesn't mean causation: court filings by the owner of the building show that Kanye was failing to pay rent. He owed around $65,000.

Yes, Kanye had lost one and a half billion dollars when Adidas severed ties. Still, that left him with half a billion, give or take, so it's a mystery why he didn't just pay the rent at his office. Or the water bill that I found tucked into the gate of this mansion, leaving every tap dry.

Instead the Yeezy office now found itself in a church's modest classrooms, with cracked lino floor tiles and paint peeling from the doors.

Antoinette wasn't happy. Kanye had screwed over Pastor Ron.

'You should dob on Kanye to Pastor Ron,' she said. 'He rented out the classrooms to Kanye because he loves children. But you've found out Kanye's not using them to educate children.'

Furthermore, Mark reckons he'll be kicked out of the church car park because by-laws prohibit encampments within the vicinity of schools. Except, as I saw with my own eyes, it's not a school! Mark will be moved on, not for the sake of children needing a good Christian education, but for hypebeasts and their mood boards and their Balenciaga pants.

My head falls deeper into Kanye's pillow. I realise I've snookered myself. I need to write a book that grapples with moral quandaries, like the ones raised by the plight of Mark. But I don't have a leg to stand on. No matter what I dig up, revealing the dubious behaviour of others, readers will be like: *You've broken into a stranger's house, you're sleeping in a stranger's bed, and you've downed your fourth bottle of a stranger's sake.*

I'm the least sympathetic character in a story. Which, keep in mind, features a Hitler enthusiast.

I put on my glasses and peek out the window. I can make out the lookout deck on the hill across the road, and it seems to be imp-free. The coast is clear. I decide to return to the kitchen in the blue mansion.

SAFFRON

I came for sake but, grabbing a bottle from the fridge, I spot a row of jars of dried pasta on a shelf. Each is labelled. 'Penne.' I've heard of that. But it soon rolls into the unfamiliar. 'Farfalle', 'Orzo', 'Ziti', 'Orecchiette', 'Cavatappi', 'Gemelli', 'Strozzapreti', 'Mezze Maniche', 'Elbow'.

Elbow?

I'm drawn to this jar. It speaks to me. The elbow connects dem bones. I need to eat dinner, and it's perfect. I scoot to the pantry. We'll infuse dem bones pasta with saffron. It'll be a nice break from beef jerky and Egg McMuffins.

I'm winging this recipe, but basically it's about steeping, and I've steeped before. I pull a pot from a hook on the wall and rest it on the stovetop. The taps aren't working because Kanye won't pay his water bill, so using a mug I scoop water out of the bucket accepting the drip. Ten trips later, I have enough water to boil the elbows in the pot. I rootle around for a mortar and pestle. I crush some saffron – one hundred dollars' worth, two hundred, who knows? I find a tablespoon and scoop warm water from the pot into a china bowl, covering the saffron. I leave the saffron to steep and the elbows to cook.

I'm exhausted. I sit down on the floor of the kitchen, the jar of saffron in my lap.

Why am I called Safran?

There is a sliver of land in the Middle East that two peoples claim is theirs, insisting history backs them. That label on the jar – *Saffron* – and the fogginess of what my family name means tells that story in its own way.

The name comes from the Arabic word za'faran, which in turn comes from the Persian word za'feran. It's the spice harvested from a flowering plant called the saffron crocus. The word goes back thousands of years.

So why am *I* called Safran? I've heard two explanations. In one my family were, long ago, spice farmers, harvesting saffron around the area now designated Israel and Palestine. In this version of events, I'm indigenous to that region. In the other explanation, my family – Jews rooted in Eastern Europe for pretty much forever – had hair as red as the threads plucked from the saffron crocus, striking, and unusual for Jews. So others began calling them Safran, which became the family name. In this version of events, I'm not indigenous to that sliver of land in the Middle East.

Holding up the jar of saffron, I realise the United Nations could adjudicate the Israel–Palestine conflict based on my family's origin story.

'They were spice farmers, the land belongs to us,' cries the Israeli ambassador.

'They had red locks, the land is ours,' rebuts the Palestinian ambassador.

Months after I leave the mansion, Israeli MMA fighter Haim Gozali posts on social media a photo of missiles to be fired into Gaza, one of them with a message written on it in Sharpie: 'Kanye West flying to Gaza'.

Haim's train of thought was: Kanye doesn't like Jews, therefore Kanye would hate being involved in an action in support of Israel, therefore I'm transforming Kanye into a Zionist in the form of a missile.

Of course, despite Haim wanting payback against Kanye, it wasn't Kanye on the receiving end of that missile. It was Palestinians.

I hear a hiss and look up. The pot of elbows is bubbling over, water spilling onto the stovetop. Time to eat.

In need of fresh air, this time I'm careful to avoid the shards of glass on the patio. I boost myself up and out, a nimble balancing act when you're bringing along a bowl of pasta. I pace around at the edge of the woods, scooping elbows into my mouth.

I've been so naive. Yes, people follow the edict that a white person can't be seen to screw over a Black person, but when the time comes, they'll weaponise another cultural fault line to try to turn everyone against me.

Like Zionist leader David Ben-Gurion sailing to Palestine in 1906, encroaching on land that wasn't his, Mr Safran finds his own West Bank – Mr West's land – not in Canaan but in Calabasas. Indulging the idea that he is following in the footsteps of gonzo writers, he fails to see that, in fact, he is carrying the flame for Zionism, continuing the ugly practice of turning up and settling a piece of land, woe upon whoever was there first. A gonZIO!

I know it sounds like I'm clowning, but I bet you twenty shekels my enemies will try on a version of that. Hey, guys, don't get too cocky, considering your situation.

In Melbourne, some people put signs on their houses that say 'We Acknowledge The Wurundjeri People as the Traditional Owners of This Land'. So, for a documentary, I dropped off some Wurundjeri people at a house with one of those signs. They rang the bell and asked if they could have the house. The residents politely declined to return the land.

The colonising of Calabasas didn't begin two nights ago, when I crossed over the stream. There's a history to this sliver of land, too.

THE HISTORY OF THE KANYE WEST BANK

One week before I entered the mansion, at a nature reserve in Calabasas, Antoinette was pulling focus on her camera, capturing a vulture perched on a rock. So far that morning she had snapped a squirrel, a rabbit and two weasels, their heads popping out of the dirt.

I was sitting on a bench nearby, under a tree, with Puchuk Ya'ia'c, a Chumash Elder. He had long grey hair and a t-shirt emblazoned with *P-22*, the name of a 'celebrity' mountain lion who prowled beneath the Hollywood sign at night.

'We're in Chumash territory here,' he said. 'The Chumash people have been here for over 13,000 years.' Spanish settlers and missionaries showed up in the late 1700s, renaming the place Calabasas.

Back then, the indigenous population of California was 300,000, with the Chumash making up between ten and twenty thousand of that.

'When the missions were established, we started to die off

dramatically. We were overworked, underfed and exposed to diseases. So half of Californian Indians did not survive the mission period, which was about sixty years.'

I didn't know what to say. It seemed obnoxious not to respond, but equally obnoxious to break the silence.

'The Catholic church only acknowledges half the truth,' Puchuk went on. 'The Pope will tell you that tribal people lost their lives during the mission period because they couldn't fight off chickenpox, mumps and measles. But they leave out the fact that we were the slave-labour force at the missions.'

Around the late 1830s, a Catholic mission granted land to three Chumash families. One of these families was Puchuk's ancestors.

'A nice chunk of land, 4400 acres.'

You'd think this was a silver lining to the cloud. Unfortunately, the Catholic missionaries were not the only powerbrokers in California. There were also politicians.

'They went to them – the three families – and said, "You guys owe taxes on this land." And they go, "We have no money." "Well, then we're going to take the land."'

As quickly as the land had been returned by the Catholic missionaries, it was snatched back by the government. But in this history of slavery and landgrabs, the equal-worst was yet to come.

'The majority of the people in California do not know about this. The first governor of this state, Peter Burnett, proclaimed he was going to exterminate all Californian Indians. And he set up a bounty system.'

This could not be further from a merely academic matter for Puchuk.

'My great-grandfather was born in 1849. When he was a little boy, a young child, a young man – up until the 1870s, someone could have killed him and they wouldn't have been sent to jail. White citizens would go out and hunt us like we were deer. If they killed us and scalped us and brought in the scalp, they got a small bounty. If they killed us and chopped our head off, they got a larger bounty, because that was better evidence.'

The politicians didn't just leave this work to vigilantes. They established the California State Militia Cavalry.

'Most Californians don't know there were over three hundred massacres here. They would wipe out whole villages, killed everybody – babies, old people. By the end of the 1800s, the tribal population across California had dropped from 300,000 to less than 20,000.'

Narrowing matters down to the Chumash of Calabasas, he said the 1900 census showed only a few hundred Chumash people were left alive.

'We went almost to extinction, and now we're here. There are now 4000 people with Chumash heritage today. We're revitalising and having a renaissance.'

There is still unfinished business.

'Universities in California have cardboard boxes. And in those cardboard boxes are Native American bones and human remains.'

More bones.

'And they keep them so they can do studies. No, no, no. You guys can't keep those. You've got to give them back. I was part of one of the largest burials in Californian history, about two miles down the road. We buried over a thousand ancient Chumash remains.'

I tried to lead the witness into denouncing Kanye for setting up a mansion on Chumash land, without following indigenous protocol. I thought it might take the heat off me for squatting there, which I was preparing to do in a week's time.

'In our belief we'd say, "When you started construction on this mansion, Kanye, did you bless and smudge the land? And make an offering, and ask the ancestors of the people that have lived here before for permission to build your compound?"'

I was hearing what I wanted to hear. But, as Puchuk went on, he sounded less like he was talking about Kanye and more like he was talking about someone else.

'You're not going to go up to the door, if this was someone's home, and open the door, and go in their house. No, you knock on their door, and you wait for someone to answer the door and invite you in. It's just simple common courtesy.'

My mouth dropped open. I asked what happened to a person who went into a house without an invitation.

'Bad things happen to you if you are disrespectful. Chumash believe there's three levels to the world. The upper world, where the sky people live. The middle world, where we are at. And the underworld. And the underworld is supernatural, scary things – scary things, scary beings, come out at night.'

'Really? Literally? Or is that an allegory?'

He brushed his grey hair from his ear.

'Calabasas is an Indian burial ground.'

BAD THINGS HAPPEN IF YOU'RE DISRESPECTFUL

Having finished my dinner of saffron elbows, I washed the bowl in the bucket accepting the drip and have now returned to Kanye's bed in the two-storey house.

Puchuk Ya'ia'c gifted me a book filled with Chumash folktales, which I'm making my way through. One story in particular is speaking to me. It warns of the consequences of taking what's not yours.

A man scales a mountain and steals the eggs of a buzzard. The buzzard decides to offer the thief a gift that will grant him great power, in exchange for the return of the eggs. Unbeknownst to the thief (but known to the buzzard), these powers expire after twelve years, at which point he dies and is claimed by the devil.

So the moral of the tale, for me, is not so much that you'll be punished for your misdeeds, but that you can delude yourself – for twelve whole years! – that not only have you not been punished, you've been rewarded for your crimes.

I'm antsy about this folktale because – arguably – I crossed another boundary this morning. I can't tell if I did. On the one hand, it's different to the situation with the elbows and the bottles of sake. They were there and now they're not. This isn't like that. I'm still holding the item at the heart of this matter in my fingers.

Keep in mind I wasn't searching for this. To be fair to me. In my defence. It was just there, laid out on the dresser in one of the small blue rooms, off the blue hallway, over in the mansion. So, yes, I have moved it from the mansion to this house. But I haven't *taken* it. There were documents spread out on the dresser, too, and not only did I not take any of those, I didn't even read them. One even had a stamp from the United States District Court, but I left that document alone too.

But *this*, this was like a talisman. I didn't find it; it found me. It practically jumped at me from the dresser.

And now it's here with me in bed. I hold it up and it gleams, catching the moonlight coming in from the window.

Kanye West's credit card.

I brush my finger over the raised letters of his name.

How does this work? I'm only asking in theory. Just curious. If I take this with me when I leave the mansion, can I just tap it down on the card reader at Calabasas McDonald's?

What's happening to me? Why am I thinking this? Over the course of this trip I've kept pushing and pushing. And you, reader, aren't even across everything yet. Yes, you know I snuck into the Donda Academy in Simi Valley. And you know I snuck into this mansion. But there was another house in between.

HIDDEN HILLS

I was not going to let Beck slip through my fingers like I had with Elvis Costello. Antoinette's friend from her school days, synth-pop singer Alex Cameron, had a residency at a lounge bar in LA. Famous people were here to catch him. Or at least two. Singer and actress Willow Smith, who I knew to be the daughter of Will Smith from DJ Jazzy Jeff & the Fresh Prince, and Beck, who floated my boat on two counts: singer/songwriter behind 1994 hit 'Loser', and dabbler in Scientology.

He wore a black coat with black bellbottom trousers and was ordering a drink at the marble counter of the art deco bar. I leant in. 'The only thing I was going to ask you was, because Kanye – didn't he rush on stage at a ceremony when you were there?' Antoinette had briefed me on this incident moments before. I was more across his Scientology years.

'Yeah,' Beck said. 'He came up on stage to take my award away when I won the Grammy. Then later he did a whole thing. "He didn't deserve it and it should have been Beyoncé."'

This was Kanye's lesser-known sequel to the infamous Taylor Swift incident in 2009, when he had grabbed the microphone from her while she was accepting an MTV Award, making his opinion known that nominee Beyoncé should have prevailed.

In 2015, Beck won the Grammy for Album of the Year, a category in which Beyoncé had been also nominated.

'He called my ex-wife,' Beck told me. 'My ex-wife was getting her hair cut, and one of the Kardashians was next to her and just handed her the phone. And then he said, "I apologise to you."'

Beck said he wasn't offended by Kanye storming the stage in the first place, but he was confused by Kanye apologising to his ex-wife.

One of Antoinette's American friends, Sedona, was also at the bar. Antoinette regaled her with the tale of us being chased from a church by Moonface and Kanye's hypebeasts.

'Kanye's got a house in Hidden Hills,' Sedona told us. 'Have you guys been inside there?'

'No, because it's a gated community,' Antoinette said. 'We've tried.'

We had called a realtor who was selling a house in Hidden Hills, claiming we were interested in the property. The realtor said we'd need to furnish her with various financial documents – basically proof we were squillionaires – before she could show the house. The average home behind those gates goes for $8.5 million, with a top one going for $40 million.

'If you want to go in, a bunch of my best friends live there,' Sedona offered.

'Can we?'

'Yeah. I'll get you in there. It's its own town – it has its own zip code.'

DRAKE'S

The security guard sat in the booth, controlling the boom gate. The wooden archway framing the entrance showed a silhouette of a cowboy on a horse above iron lettering: *Hidden Hills*.

Most of the vehicles making their way in were those of labourers. We waited patiently in the queue. Sedona's friend had put us on a list. We showed our IDs, the guard found us on a sheet on his clipboard, and then he waved us through the gate.

Massive sycamore trees lined the street. We crawled along, trying to understand the place. Even though it was just a short drive from the cement and honks of downtown LA, the neighbourhood had a bemusing stillness to it, a pastoral haven: 650 houses spread over 4.5 square kilometres. I had no idea where all those labourers had disappeared to, and I couldn't spot many residents either. Occasionally pairs of horseback riders trotted by. I don't believe they were off to herd cattle.

Sedona had sketched directions for us on a piece of paper, but she didn't know Kanye's exact house number, so Antoinette dropped me off somewhere in the vicinity.

In an otherwise silent street, chatter was coming through an open door, so I wandered over and gave a gentle knock. A man with no flaws, not even a wrinkle in his shirt, came to the door. I held up the Yemulke, wrapped in bubble wrap, and said I had a package for Kanye West. He pointed to the house next door, but I could see he immediately realised something was off and regretted imparting that information.

I made my way to the large, but not ridiculously enormous, cream home next door. I knocked and no one answered. But I knew this was Kanye's place. I'd never been surer of anything. Because hanging from the doorknob was a cardboard sign from the water company that read 'Notice of Intent to Disconnect'.

I hopped back in the Jeep and we drove on. Kim Kardashian owned a home here too, but we couldn't even get close. She lived in a gated community within the gated community. I giggled; for Kim, even in Hidden Hills there was a wrong side of the tracks.

Antoinette hadn't given up, winding slowly through the streets and pulling up outside another mansion. According to her research, this was Drake's.

She told me to check if Drake was home. That the Black Canadian rapper was Jewish, so he would *get* the Yemulke. In fact, he was probably furious at Kanye for his Hitler talk. I could pass on the mantle – Drake could be the one to confront Kanye with the Yemulke, using it as a conversation starter.

I was struggling to pull the threads together. But it made more sense than asking Pastor Ron to ask Kanye to baptise me, so it was good enough for now. I rolled out of the Jeep and headed to Drake's gate, a rustic metal door cut into a tall wooden fence.

The door was secured by a heavy wrought-iron latch. Or it would have been, if the latch had been locked. I squeaked the gate open, and the lacklustre security immediately made sense. A dozen workers were busy in the yard – they would need to get in and out.

Getting my bearings, I realised this was the rear entrance. The property was massive. Walking further in, I found a house to either side of me, and neither was even *the* house! (One was a guesthouse, the other an office, I later read on a realtor's website.) And the house was not even a house – it was a Southern French *estate*. Two-storeys of stone, looking yellow in this light, vines crawling all over, with grand, oversized arch windows.

It was going be quite the walk to the back door. A bulldozer was tearing up the earth. In fact, with the exception of several modern-art sculptures and an unusually shaped swimming pool, the whole yard was a vast square of mud. Presumably they were midway through a landscaping project.

I started my way through, resigned to the fact my New Balances would be caked in mud by the time I reached Drake's back door.

The workers didn't pay me any attention. I was waiting for one of them to say something – I wanted them to – so I could ask in return if Drake was home. That I had a delivery. But no one said anything. Before I knew it I was standing at the foot of a staircase that led to a second-storey entrance. Surely while climbing these stairs one of the workers would call out something along the lines of, *Can we help you?* But they didn't. Was I a ghost? With only a few steps to go,

I could see the door was open and could hear chatting from within. I couldn't see who the chatterers were, though.

Now I had walked through the doorway. I was standing in Drake's back entrance hall. It was white, marble and empty. On the other side of the hall were two doors, presumably leading to different parts of the estate. Mind-fuckingly, the moment – the very second – I stepped into this hall, one of those two doors clicked shut, so I missed whoever was there, chatting, only moments before.

I decided to try the other door first. While this was frightening, in the moment it felt less scary than opening the door leading to the chatterers. Despite possibly being invisible, I was vibrating with fear.

The door opened onto the landing of a staircase leading down to the ground floor. The walls were light grey stone, like in a castle. I made my way down the stairs to an atrium; archways in all directions led to palatial rooms, with walnut floors and double-height ceilings. A billiards room, with black felt stretched over the table, and a piano nearby; a dining room, with a long, varnished table surrounded by twelve orange-brown leather chairs.

Back in the atrium I came across an art piece, which hip-hop heads might like. Behind glass, *MAD* magazines, tagged with silver markers, mimicking the graffiti on trains. Next to this, a framed oil painting of a young Black man.

I made my way through the atrium and reached a kitchen. There I was slapped by the reality of where I was and what I was doing. Explaining to someone why you're unexpectedly standing in their backyard is very different to explaining why you're standing in their kitchen.

I walked across the kitchen to a counter where a row of family photos sat in matching gold frames. In the first one, a young bride and groom were kissing at their garden wedding. Both were white. The next photo along showed the bride surrounded by six bridesmaids. All white. The next photo along, a family of six, standing around the piano I just saw in the billiards room. Caucasian, Caucasian, Caucasian, Caucasian, Caucasian and Caucasian.

I knew it was time to ghost.

Safely outside the back gate, looking out to the street, I saw Antoinette waiting in the Jeep. A worker, ignoring me, was about to enter the gate.

'Hello,' I said.

He smiled and said hello back.

I held up the Yemulke wrapped in bubble wrap.

'I've got a delivery from a colleague of Drake's. And I was told this was the address. But maybe I've got the wrong address.'

'Drake?' He pointed to the house next door. 'That's his house.'

'Oh.'

'But he sold it a year ago.'

He walked through the gate and creaked it shut.

NEW UNBALANCE

I set down Kanye's credit card on Kanye's bedside table and tuck myself into his bed.

I spent longer in the Drakeless house than I thought. I know this because I pulled out my phone after I bade farewell to the worker and saw Antoinette had left a string of messages.

Where are you?
I hear a lot of screaming. What's going on??????
Jesus Christ. What the hell is going on?
Are you alive???

Driving out of Hidden Hills, I turned to her. 'You're anxious. Why?'

'Because you keep putting yourself at risk by trespassing into properties. I don't know what's going on. You say you're just knocking on a door – it turns out you're trespassing in someone's home, with security cameras everywhere. You're very comfortable with it, but you shouldn't be. And the more you're doing it, the more comfortable you're getting.'

I ruminate on this, rolling to one side, sinking into the mattress. Am I turning into that man? Have I *already* turned into him? Am I no longer the guy who interviews the cranks? Have I become the crank?

THAT MAN: DAVID COLE

One of the lenses in David Cole's glasses was cracked. I had reached out to him because he had defended Kanye after he was accused of antisemitism, and he asked to meet in the bar at Mr. C, a five-star hotel in Beverly Hills. We moved from the opulent inside bar – old-world leather couches, soft lighting catching every knot in the wood panels – to the more casual terrace, looking out to the hotel driveway, even though it was not the weather for it.

'I love this overcast, rainy stuff we've been having, because we're overdue for it and I want to savour it,' David said. He held up his champagne flute. 'L'chaim.'

'L'chaim.'

'I have one and a half to two litres of straight liquor a day.'

I dug deep for my *not-judging* voice. 'Like, vodka and stuff?'

'Rum, because it's cheaper. If it were up to me, I would drink whiskey or brandy, but rum is simply cheaper here. Right across the street there, you can get two litres of rum for $10.99.'

Like me, he came to drinking late. He discovered it in his thirties – a cure for his chronic insomnia.

'I realised I just prefer wandering through the world drunk. I think it's perhaps a symptom of some latent hostility towards the world.'

I came here to discuss Kanye, but found I wanted to know more about David. I didn't have to broach any awkward subjects, he came out with it all unprompted.

'I mean, the same reason ... these glasses have been broken for over a year. I have the money to get them fixed. People say to me, why don't you get the glasses fixed? And I'm like, well, I like showing my disdain for the world by walking around drunk with broken glasses.'

A Rolls-Royce crawled up the hotel driveway.

'This is a very pricey joint,' he said.

Indeed, it was. I said I'd buy the drinks and he ordered a Bellini, a notably expensive cocktail. This makes me sound like a jerk, but I thought to myself: seeing you're an alcoholic, can't you go with something a bit cheaper?

David had lived quite the life. The more he told me about himself, the more I knew Kanye could wait. He wanted to keep the prickliest bit of his life separate from his other work, his other beliefs.

He was a Holocaust Revisionist, a person who thought the number of Jews murdered in the Holocaust, according to the official and widely accepted history, was exaggerated. This would be an uneasy subject on its own. But there was more. His 'l'chaim' before wasn't cultural appropriation. David was Jewish.

And it all began because, as a young man, he was driven by the same impulses that drove me. He was a stickybeak, a writer and filmmaker, drawn to the same worlds I was drawn to.

'When I got out of high school, I wanted to be a filmmaker, as everybody here does.' He gestured across the LA skyline. 'What had fascinated me was extreme human ideology. And I began contacting every ideological organisation in LA and going to meet with them, chat with them. It took me to the 35-years-ago version of Antifa, left-wing riot groups. And it took me to some of the most far-right racist groups. I was not a believer in any of it. I was just studying their belief.'

So far, so Safran.

'But then I encountered one guy who made me curious.'

The guy, David McCalden, a British-born American, ran a Holocaust Revisionist think-tank in Los Angeles.

'And after months of spending many an afternoon having tea with David McCalden, I came to the conclusion that there were some things that needed to be looked into about the Holocaust narrative.'

David Cole turned his focus from me to the server wandering the terrace. 'I would like another Bellini, please.'

He jumped on a plane, filmed a documentary at Polish concentration camps and annoyed the director of the Auschwitz-Birkenau State Museum; his writing, too, turned to questioning the official story. Word spread across the American Jewish community. In 1991, he turned up to UCLA to give a speech. Jewish groups were waiting. Most unnervingly for David, one of these groups was the Jewish Defense League, who would later be classified as a terrorist organisation by the FBI.

'I didn't realise just how much they were going to oppose me being there. So I show up on that day. I'm all by myself. I didn't bring security. And I see about three hundred angry people coming towards the stage. And they're chanting and they're screaming, and they have placards against me. I was pelted with food. And then when that didn't drive me away, a guy from the Jewish Defense League jumped on the stage and started punching me in the face.'

I was feeling bad that I had whined, in my head, about him ordering the expensive cocktails. His stories were more than worth it. And I sensed bespoke wisdom was coming. I picked up the menu and asked if he wanted to eat. The thin-sliced yellowtail? He was happy to stick with drinks.

Ducking the final punches, he fled the stage at UCLA. But it wasn't over. The Jewish Defense League put a $25,000 bounty on his head. Although he had clearly, so far, survived the threat of the bounty – here he was, before my eyes, beckoning the server for a third Bellini.

Did he still have to sleep with one eye open, with this price on his head?

'No, I'm free to say whatever I want. They're dead. They're all dead. Irv Rubin and Earl Krugel ran the Jewish Defense League.'

I knew I had come to discuss Kanye, but I needed to hear more.

'Krugel was the one who punched me at that speech. Both went to jail after 9/11. They had been caught planning to blow up a mosque in California and assassinate a Lebanese-American congressman.'

Earl Krugel pleaded guilty. A few years later, a white-supremacist prisoner crushed his head with a concrete block, killing him. Meanwhile, Irv Rubin, in the words of David Cole, 'took a nosedive five storeys down, straight on his head' while awaiting trial.

David Cole, another Jewish writer and filmmaker who liked to push his luck. We were both into our third Bellinis, the prosecco and peach-nectar cocktails taking their effect. My fingers slipped on the stem of the champagne flute, splashing the drink onto my New Balance sneakers. I glanced across and noticed David Cole was wearing New Balance too. Although his were falling apart, with a little of his toe poking through.

David survived the Jewish Defense League but not the social stigma of going too far, quibbling about the Holocaust. He changed his name in the late nineties, reinventing himself, and started running one of LA's largest Republican organisations. 'Republican Party Animals' recast the Republicans as fresh, fun and driven by the kind of libertarian values that Hollywood types were into. He was the toast of the town, clinking flutes of Bellini with stars like Clint Eastwood, Tom Selleck, Jerry Bruckheimer and Kristy Swanson, the original Buffy the Vampire Slayer. He continued being a writer and filmmaker, but now a respectable one, with a growing audience and work published in the *Wall Street Journal* and the *Hollywood Reporter*.

Then an ex-girlfriend snitched. An explosive 2013 article in the *Guardian* revealed that Republican Party darling David Stein was in fact Holocaust Revisionist David Cole. He said everyone deserted him. Friends, colleagues, his audience. Now, in 2023, he was looking at me through a cracked lens, with his toe pushing through his sneaker.

David had been in a state of delusion that a gadfly, a gonzo – a snoop with a pen – could just do anything and people would come along for the ride. But clearly people draw the line at denying the Holocaust. But what about trespassing?

Antoinette's right, I'm desensitised to the reality of what I'm doing. No one's going to be like, *Those Hidden Hills hypocrites! Hollywood liberals lecture us about equality, yet they live in a gated community!* No, nobody's going to think that. They're going to be like, *Jeepers, imagine if I walked into my kitchen at night and there's John Safran at the kitchen table, digging into a tub of ice cream.*

And couldn't there just as easily have been a third man sitting with David and me on the terrace, sipping Bellinis? Another grown man convinced everyone would just go along with their transgressive creative impulses, no matter what. Only to find out the hard way that this wasn't the case. Although the man I'm thinking of wouldn't have been wearing New Balance – he would have been in Yeezys.

'I JUST PREFER WANDERING THROUGH THE WORLD DRUNK'

I was too desensitised to everything. I was buying drinks for a Holocaust Revisionist, convinced I could have explained it to my grandmother if she was alive. *I'm learning from the Holocaust Revisionists. Not the bad things, Bubbe. Other things – things that will help with my book.* Yes. She would have bragged to her bridge buddies that her grandson had a book, and not worried about the Holocaust Revisionist running up his bar tab.

There must be something to David's creative process – wandering through the world drunk with a cracked lens – because he told me something I had never thought about before: Jewish and Black Americans were at odds because they occupied the same space in the culture.

The two groups had a history of banding together in both politics and the arts. But *why* had they banded together? David took me through a couple of conventional explanations offered by others, which he felt only told part of the story.

The first conventional explanation was that both Jewish and Black people were minorities, so they held empathy for each other and teamed up to fight back against bigots. This wasn't just feel-good hyperbole. According to one figure, two thirds of the white people involved in the Freedom Riders era of civil rights activism were Jewish.

In 1964, less than 7 per cent of Black Mississippians who were eligible to vote were actually registered. Civil rights activists said this was because Black people were dissuaded from registering, in both subtle and extreme ways. In June that year, a Black church that had been running a registration campaign was burnt down. Three civil rights activists came from out of town to investigate the suspicion that the Ku Klux Klan was responsible. The Klan was tipped off about the trio, and conspired with local law enforcement to deal with them. The three young men, all in their early twenties, were pulled over and forced out of the car. Each was shot through the heart. One was a Black Mississippian, the other two were New York Jews.

David now took me through another explanation of why Jewish and Black Americans found themselves bound together. In this version of events, Jewish people noticed there were Black art forms, like hip-hop, yet to be discovered by a mainstream audience. So they encroached into this space, with an eye out for a buck: Jewish rappers like the Beastie Boys, and Jewish record-label bosses like Rick Rubin.

But David proposed a third explanation. This was the one I'd never heard before.

'I think the thing that Blacks and Jews share in common, number one: we're both verbal people. In terms of people who have high verbal skills, there's probably no group on earth more verbal than Blacks and Jews.'

I could see it. Hip-hop, from Public Enemy to Kanye, is the wordiest of musical forms, bending and playing with language. And Jewish American comedy – Groucho Marx, Lenny Bruce – is the same. I remember working after-hours in an office in 1990. *Seinfeld* was blasting from a television across the hall. And even though I couldn't see the screen, I was still cracking up; it was all words, words, words.

This proclivity to play with language was David's explanation of why the two groups ended up in the same spaces in America. What others considered being too loud, Jews and Blacks thought was just the right volume.

I loved this. It broadened the idea of what brings people together to something beyond political views, race, creed or even the shared experience of having to run from the Klan.

'Blacks and Jews are masters of word play, and we are entertainers. We are the people who pretty much created US entertainment.'

This was good. This was a happy ending. Rick Rubin got in with LL Cool J, Run DMC and Public Enemy – my teenage favourites, all Black – not to exploit them, but because he admired their artistry, their rhyme flow. Hip-hop is amazing, American comedy and cinema is amazing, and both Black and Jewish Americans were integral to it all. The end. Picking away at positive things until the Jews look bad is for the hard right and hard left, not me.

DAY THREE AT THE McMANSION

This morning, five Egg McMuffins sit on the bridge on my side of the gate. I unwrap one.

Pastor Ron doesn't shoot animals and never has

Cryptic. I unwrap another.

His father was a vet

An army vet or an animal vet? Is this going somewhere? I try another.

I'll be out of range for the next 24 hours because I'm going to a shooting range. I have befriended Pastor Ron

I see Antoinette has got over her worry about American gun culture. And then:

I went to a gun shop with him and I met some of the nicest people. All MAGA people. Did you know Justin Trudeau is Fidel Castro's son? A Canadian in the gun store told me that

I grimace. Still not clear on which type of vet Pastor Ron's dad is.

Finally:

Let me know if you see any rabbits

I walk back up the bridge, ring the doorbell on the cottage behind the garage again (Kanye doesn't answer), and end up on the far side of the two-storey mansion. I've placed a large plastic tub out here to catch rainwater, which I use to fill up the empty sake bottles with drinking water. I'm not feeling thirsty, but looking at my five Egg McMuffins, I better grab one.

I do have a book to write as part of my writer's residency here. Let's not forget that. It's clear the mansion wants me out – two more skylights have burst open in the big blue room. But that's exactly why I should push through and stay. I should write from somewhere I don't belong. Except I would need to sit in a soaked office chair or in a puddle on the floor. And Kanye's bedroom? That house is trying to suffocate me with the smell of slept-in sheets and my own feet. I'm left with no choice but to flee.

Obviously my feet have come with me, but it's different out here in the fresh air, sitting cross-legged in the woods, with a tablecloth I found in the house wrapped around me. I've made sure to plant myself away from the toilet holes I dig each morning. I'm deep enough in the woods so neither the mansion nor the imp in the lookout can spot me, a strap of beef jerky dangling from my mouth.

I've brought *Pocket Guide to Animal Tracks* and *California Plants: A guide to our iconic flora*; I haven't spotted any animals, but the plant names alone are warnings that I shouldn't get too comfortable. The jagged-leafed plant next to me is called coyote brush, and to my other side the white puffs on stalks are bear grass. Why couldn't

DAY THREE AT THE McMANSION

I have got the gentler sounding rabbitbrush and deerweed, which are also listed in the book?

You can walk through a city and never look up, missing the intricate second-storey facades from days of old that sit above the 7-Elevens and Chemist Warehouses. But one day you spot them, and from then on they're always part of your urban scenery. I'm learning that my ears do a similar thing. It's only on this third day that they have attuned to nature; for the first time I'm hearing animal sounds, which surely have been here since I turned up. It's the most benign of these that's messing with my head, because as I'm typing and typing in the woods, all I can hear are crickets. The universal signal that no one's laughing at your joke.

YE

Pastor Ron's office was on the other side of the church from the classrooms the Yeezy hypebeasts had filled with mood boards, clothing samples, piles of shoes and boots, and photographs of Kanye's wife. While he had handed over to the Spanish-language congregation, he was yet to pack up his belongings here for his big move to Arizona.

Antoinette was setting up her easel. He was set to come in soon, delighted that Antoinette wanted to paint him. I stretched out on the couch, and, among the office fare, spotted a box, flaps open, filled with Twinkies.

'It's really pouring down outside,' I said. 'If we're lucky, we'll be trapped in here with the Yeezy staff and we can exchange Twinkies for revelations.'

Pastor Ron came up the hallway on an electric scooter, presumably because, with all his injuries, even short walks hurt. Antoinette welcomed him into his own office, setting him in a lounge chair near the window.

'The three most stressful things in life are a death, divorce and moving,' he said, as she fidgeted with the venetian blinds until the light hit his face just so. He had lost his brother to fentanyl, he'd been through a divorce, and was presently packing up his house, which sat next door to the church.

'I am ready for a new adventure. I never even had to list my house, put it on the market.'

This was because of Kanye.

'Ye, he is looking at the back building of the church, and he says, "What about that?" I said, "Well, that's on my property, we're not leasing that." And, long story short, he ends up buying my house.'

'Did you get more because he was desperate to buy it?' I asked, hoping for a scandal.

'Nah.' Kanye paid what anyone else would have paid.

Disappointed by the lack of scandal, I tried peeking at the portrait in progress, but Antoinette shooed me away.

'I have a period where the painting just goes to hell. And then, if I can be patient, I can resolve it. So I'm going to rely on that. Just have to.'

Pastor Ron asked us what our biggest fears were. Antoinette: being alone; Pastor Ron: something happening to his kids; John: spiders. Then he asked us what our most romantic moments had been.

'I've only been in love one time – my first girlfriend,' Pastor Ron said. 'In West Virginia there's this cave called Hellhole. An opening in the ground that goes down through a chute 300 feet, then it flares out into a great big room, a pit, called the Tower of Babel. And we had done it and climbed out. It was the dead of night. We set up our tent on the edge of this really nice field. And we woke up in the snow and just spent the day in the tent eating oatmeal raisin cookies.'

He looked to me. 'John?'

'I remember walking, this morning, by the waterfall.'

'You didn't find that romantic,' Antoinette said.

'There was a waterfall though, a little one.'

'He's lying. He didn't care about the waterfall. I did.'

I excused myself and left the room.

Midafternoon, midweek, the place was lifeless. Not even Mark was around.

I dawdled down the other hallway, but it appeared to be a day off for the hypebeasts. I poked my head out of the entrance of the church building. It was bucketing down. No Moonface, or anyone else, guarding the gate that led to the back of the church. Now that my ears thought about it, no squealing of power tools from the construction site, either.

I ducked into the bathroom for only a minute. But when I came out the atmosphere had totally changed. The car park was bustling. Cars were pulling up, parents and kids pouring out of vehicles. Everyone was outfitted in black – shirts, pants, dresses, shoes. One woman sported a black kaftan, and when she turned to shut her car door I saw 'YE 2024' printed on the back. These weren't members of the new congregation, they were the Donda Academy kids and their parents.

Catching my reflection in one of the foyer's floor-to-ceiling windows, I realised my inclination to dress in Melbourne black matched the occasion. Without thinking too hard about it, I started welcoming people, ushering them in through the foyer and to the church sanctuary; lots of mutual hellos and head nods. They took me to be a security guy. A man asked for the restrooms and I pointed him the right way.

Once the parents were seated, a choir of children sang in Latin on the stage of the church sanctuary. Then an adult – I wasn't sure of his exact role in the Donda Academy – stood up and addressed the parents. I scanned the room for Kanye, but no dice. I remained at the sanctuary door, keeping up the facade that I was one of Kanye's security men.

In my dream scenario, this Donda Academy leader would preach like the grand poobah of a cult or secret society, all their explosive esoteric doctrines unveiled to an outsider – me! – for the very first time. Frustratingly, from where I stood, I could only pick up skerricks of intel. He was pitching to the parents the case for teaching their children Latin, liturgical music and classical music, even if they weren't in their own cultural and artistic traditions.

I was disappointed it was sounding so reasonable. John Safran exposes reasonableness. No market for that.

Then, at last, things turned a little fiery. Having hyped up the parents, he now scolded them for being hyped up. He said that this cultural and artistic program wasn't just for fun. Both parents and students would suffer through long, gruelling hours where they'd think they couldn't take it anymore. But they must. This wasn't just a school like other schools, it was a fraternity, and they were all going to change the world.

So it did get a bit culty, but not enough for my liking.

The rain was now pelting the floor-to-ceiling windows at the entrance. A woman wearing a t-shirt that said 'Ye Must Be Born Again' was setting sandwiches out on a table in the foyer.

All of a sudden, I sensed a bad moon rising. I swivelled my head and there he was, appearing from the hallway on the Yeezy side. Moonface. He spotted me and began sprinting my way. I fled towards Pastor Ron's office, down the hallway on the non-Yeezy side. Springing through the doorway, I shut and locked the door behind me, Moonface's sausage fingers narrowly escaping the slam.

Antoinette, by the easel, looked alarmed.

'Where's Pastor Ron?' I asked her.

She told me he'd left for steak and eggs at the IHOP while she continued to work on the portrait.

We could hear the doorknob wiggling.

I explained what had gone down. She groaned, but not at me. She was over Kanye's hypebeasts and henchmen. She was over all of Kanye's antics – particularly how people like Mark, a guy who slept in his car, had become collateral damage.

'For a while I was convinced that Kanye might be a good guy because he'd helped out Mark a bit,' she said. 'I'm just disappointed that Kanye let him down, and that he used him as a pawn to get what he wanted and then dumped him after. And I feel sorry for Pastor Ron. He did not sign up for Yeezy offices to be set up here.' Antoinette suspected Kanye was breaking zoning laws doing this. 'We can look through the California law. I would love it if he was evicted. Love it.'

The doorknob was rattled more forcefully. Then came a pounding so brutal, the door shook.

I knew I had to face the music. I made my way over, unlocked the door and squeaked it open. It wasn't Moonface, it was Raphael the hypebeast, in his black streetwear.

'You have to go.'

'This is Pastor Ron's office,' Antoinette said. 'He says we can be here.'

With this piece of information he retreated, pulling his phone from his pocket.

A few minutes later, another knock. I opened the door to Raphael again.

'Yes, I called Pastor Ron. He confirmed what you said. You can stay here. But you must stay in this room. No *bumbling*.'

Watching Raphael retreat down the hallway, there he was again: Moonface, now guarding the door one room down from Pastor Ron's office. He threw a menacing glance my way.

I just knew right away. Nothing else would have made sense. I was pulling fragments of information together. The other hallway was the Yeezy hallway, so why was Moonface guarding a room on this side? And parents and kids had showed up for a big Donda Academy event. Classical music was coming from the church sanctuary.

'Kanye's here,' I said to Moonface.

He changed tack with his guarding strategy; now he was avoiding eye contact, staring ahead, but still looking like he was about to blow.

'He's in there,' I offered as a follow-up.

Moonface's complexion was looking more like Mars.

I retreated into the office.

'Kanye's in there,' I told Antoinette, pointing through the wall to the next room. 'What do I do?'

'Don't make things bad for Pastor Ron,' she said, adding another stroke to his nose.

I plucked a Twinkie from the box and paced the room. Not coming up with anything better, I made my way to the wall separating this office from the next room. I balled up my fist and gave the wall a thump.

'Hello?'

I thumped a little harder and spoke a little louder.

'Kanye?'

'Try "Ye",' Antoinette said. 'He's called Ye now.'

I set down my half-eaten Twinkie next to Antoinette's tubes of paints so I could make use of both fists.

'Ye!'

I thumped harder.

'YE! YE! YE!'

Antoinette continued painting. Now my forearms went to work along with my fists.

'YEEEEEEE! YEEEEEEEEE!'

My voice becoming hoarse, I fell to my knees and struggled on, shifting gears to a new plea: 'WHY ARE YOU DOING TORAH CLASSES?'

Did I hear something? I pushed my ear to the wall.

The world's tiniest 'ye' came through the wall.

'ye!' said the world tiniest ye. It was a mocking shout, muffled by the wall.

'He's talking!' I told Antoinette.

'What?'

'Come here.'

We both pressed our ears against the wall. I was clenching my jaw, squeezing my eyes shut, drawing in the energy from every ounce of my existence, from every nook and cranny of my anatomy, and sending it to my ears.

I couldn't hear anything.

But I had before. I promised Antoinette I had heard the world's tiniest ye. She returned to her painting.

I backed up as far as I could and took a run up, launching myself in the air. The loudest, most primal 'YE!' came from somewhere inside me as my whole body hit the wall.

I collapsed on the floor. I was breathing heavily. I needed to calm down.

A phone rang. Antoinette put down her brush and picked up the call.

'You guys have got to go,' came Pastor Ron's voice.

Antoinette packed up her easel and paints. As we made our way out, there he was, still guarding the room next to Pastor Ron's. Now he was happy to make eye contact. He was beaming with delight and self-satisfaction. I'd never seen the moon shine so bright.

TORAH CLASSES

The morning after I was thwarted by Moonface, I followed another lead. It felt like a lifetime ago, but Tamar, the Jewish educator who had helped Kanye with one of his versions of Donda Academy, had told me he was studying Torah with an Orthodox rabbi. Frustratingly, she wouldn't tittle-tattle and reveal who he was.

But I had my ways. I'd learnt the location of the rabbi in question, or at least I hoped so, strolling into this LA synagogue.

It was midmorning. A few men in black fedora-style hats and suits were chatting at a table. Strangers wander in and out of houses of worship all the time, so this was not a melodramatic moment for them. They pointed me to a doorway – the rabbi's office – and went back to chatting.

The rabbi was relaxed, too, his black hat parked among the mess of books and papers on his desk.

Orthodox rabbis come in two flavours. Those dismissive of secular Jews – *heretics* – and those who pep up when a secular

Jew walks into their office – *here's a heretic I can bring closer to God.* I sensed this rabbi was the latter, because he asked me, 'You put on tefillin today?' (Reader, we will get to what that means.)

I wanted to start by broaching the subject of Kanye, so I removed the conversation starter from my head and held it towards him.

'What do we have here?' he asked.

'A Kanye sneaker repurposed as a yarmulke.'

He broke out laughing. 'Nice!'

'A Yemulke.'

Now he knew I was here for Kanye reasons, but he didn't seem fazed at all. In fact, he called in one of the black-hatters from the synagogue and pointed. 'That's Kanye's shoe on his head!'

The black-hatter didn't laugh. He stared pensively, processing this information. 'Can I make a point?' he finally said. 'The sneaker starts at the bottom and the yarmulke's at the top.'

'That's right,' the rabbi said to me. 'What he told you is a deep concept.'

'The shoe is something that's trodden on,' the black-hatter went on. 'Very low. It's dirty and you're getting all the dust of the earth. It is linked to the foot, which is unsanctified.'

He explained that, in ancient times, the high priests were commanded to wash their feet before entering the holy temple of King Solomon.

'The feet – except for those with a fetish of some kind – the feet are kind of disgusting,' the rabbi added.

He motioned to me to pass him the Yemulke, lifting his glasses and holding it close to his face.

The black-hatter ramped it up: 'Versus something that sits on top of your head, a yarmulke. It's a crown.'

The rabbi held up the Yemulke. 'You've transformed a shoe – something low – to a crown. Wow!'

'But not a crown to brag,' the black-hatter warned. 'It signifies that there's something above us. It's an act of humility of ours to say we are not the greatest being. There is something that is above us and exists beyond us. And so that's symbolised by the yarmulke.'

The rabbi passed the Yemulke back to me and motioned to a velvet bag on his desk. 'Let's get back to it. You put on tefillin today?'

This is a standard question asked when an Orthodox Jew bumps into a secular one. This bugs some secular Jews; in the way you might be bugged if a Scientologist shoved his beliefs in your face. But I was not bugged. I loved putting on tefillin, just like I was always up for an E-Meter audit or a baptism.

From the velvet bag, the rabbi pulled out the tefillin: a hollow black cube, midway between the size of a miniature Rubik's cube and a standard one. A parchment of scripture is rolled up inside, and you wrap a leather strap around your arm seven times to bind the cube to your bicep, pointing to your heart. They come in pairs; the second black cube is attached to your forehead by a loop of leather.

As I began wrapping the leather strap around my arm, the black-hatter was revving up again. He said the tefillin's leather straps were imbued with the essence of the animal it came from. And by binding these to my arm and head, I was binding the essence of this animal to the base animal impulses within me.

'You are creating this alchemy that transcends beyond this baseness into something of great spiritual significance.'

The rabbi tried to butt in, but the black-hatter was on a roll.

'Now, the fact that you have on a Kanye sneaker transformed to a yarmulke makes this moment even greater, because we really do need the animalistic force of negativity to be transformed.'

'Moishe!' the rabbi snapped. He turned back to me. 'Kanye is one of our friends here. And we know from the Talmud that everything that goes south could go north, and everything that goes north could go south. So we start a new day every day, and we welcome everyone – even antisemites – to come and be part of the love. Because the love rubs off. You know what I'm saying?'

'For sure.'

I didn't know if the black-hatter, Moishe, had irked the rabbi simply by talking out of school or whether the rabbi felt a deeper discomfort, hearing a Black man being compared to something animalistic.

Either way, Moishe didn't catch the rabbi's drift that he should proceed with a lighter touch when talking about Kanye.

'The shtreimel,' Moishe said. 'You know a shtreimel?'

I did. It was the hat favoured by certain Orthodox rabbis; the one shaped like a big wheel of cheese covered in black fur.

'That was originally a punishment in Poland, to call out the Jews. Like a yellow star. Like, *Oh, they're the Jews, we make them wear these stupid hats.* But there's this idea, tikkun olam, and it's taking those things that are bad and negative and transforming them, turning them around. They turned around the shtreimel. You are doing the same thing. Taking the bad energy put out by Kanye and turning it into a symbol of pride and saying, screw you!'

The rabbi sighed.

Having completed the ritual, I unwrapped the black cube from my arm and lifted the other one from my forehead, passing them over the desk to the rabbi.

'You ever heard of the term divine providence?' the rabbi asked. 'In Yiddish they call it "bashert". And bashert means it was meant to be. Every moment is designed with intent, every little detail of it, even if we can't see it at the time.' He zipped the tefillin up in the velvet bag. 'Kanye came here so you would come here and put on tefillin.'

The Yemulke proved to be a conversation starter, as I'd hoped, but it wasn't a conversation keep-going-er. The rabbi kept shtum about his classes with Kanye.

PANIC ROOM ON WHEELS

Wrapped in the filthy tablecloth, I head back towards the two-storey house with the open laptop balanced on my head, the glow of the screen guiding my way. So much for the critics who would say I should have brought one of the three torches packed in my duffle bag.

I pass by the locked-up white cottage. I can't lay my eyes on it without feeling unsettled – cute facade, door with a mail slot and welcome mat. Moving further along, I reach the rear of the two-storey house, where five of Kanye's black military vehicles are parked. Four of the skeletal Polaris RZRs and another SHERP, the ominous metal box with tyres up to my neck. I can see why the Ukranians use it to cross bodies of waters and collapsed buildings.

If the imp on the hill snitches on me, if Kanye's in that white cottage, if the sheriff skids up with sirens blaring, I'm busted. They'll search the mansion, the two-storey house, maybe even the UFO ... But would they think to look in the SHERP? I assume that, even though I can't look into the blacked-out windows, I'll be able to look out.

I circle the SHERP. Weird. How do I get in? There's no driver or passenger door. Quite the brain teaser. The SHERP lacks a nose, where conventional vehicles keep their engine, but it also lacks a boot. It's an overbearing squat box. At the rear there's a black glass panel at the top and a black metal panel at the bottom. A handle sits at the dividing point.

On this adventure thus far, I've repeatedly reached out for doorhandles, assuming they won't open, and it turns out they do: the sliding doors at the patio leading into the mansion, the white door opening to the Holocaust monkeys, the classroom door in the church hallway opening to a flock of hypebeasts. I consider the handle on the back of this SHERP. I reckon it's going to open.

It does.

The handle allows me to lift the glass window until it opens ninety degrees, level with the roof of the SHERP. Having lifted the window out of the way, I can pull the metal panel down until it, too, is horizontal. I get the gist. I'm to step on a lip on the bumper, grip a bar welded to the SHERP and hoist myself into the cabin.

Before I do that, I duck up to Kanye's bedroom and retrieve a couple of quilts and a pillow, grabbing one of the Holocaust monkeys for company as I make my way out the door.

Then I make another decision. I remember there's a second SHERP, this one parked out the front of the garage, in between the blue mansion and the two-storey house. Discovering this SHERP is unlocked too, I choose this one. Because of how Kanye has parked it, I can look out and up, to monitor the imp on the hill.

PANIC ROOM ON WHEELS

The interior of the SHERP is roomier than I expected. Before I opened the back door, for all I knew the interior could have housed a king-sized engine, cogs the size of wagon wheels grinding, pistons sliding up and down, steam whistles whistling. Up front there's a driver and passenger seat, but the rear of the cabin is spacious. Bench seats run on either side, and I can tell from the canvas straps on the ceiling, like those in train carriages, that it's built to accommodate four people. And not four skinny hypebeasts – four hearty Ukrainian soldiers who grew up on a diet of potatoes and pigs, and who go out in the forest and bench-press fallen trees. The cabin is lined with padded material, patterned with army camo. In the gap between these two bench seats, there's enough floor that a person can comfortably lie down.

I slide the Holocaust monkey into the front seat and take one final look to see if anything is stirring at the lookout on the hill. Then I stretch out between the bench seats and snuggle up in Kanye's quilts.

I now realise that on the two nights I slept in Kanye's bedroom, I was under the tyranny of subconscious panic. So vulnerable to someone coming to check the place for uninvited guests. How else can I explain that I'm feeling at ease right now, more so than any time since crossing the stream? Why would the sheriff or Moonface check the SHERP? They wouldn't. It's the perfect place.

Another realisation hits. There are no mirrors in the two-storey house or the blue mansion. At least, none that I saw. Not even in the bathrooms. This must be some kooky Kanye thing, just like he insists everyone wear black. If this is the case – if he bans mirrors – he's missed one. All over this vehicle there are buttons, analogue gauges, toggles, knobs and levers. And, for some reason, a small mirror is affixed between two switches. Maybe the Ukrainian soldiers want to check if there's pig between their teeth.

For the first time in days, I can see my reflection. And I'm shocked. I'm baggy-eyed. My red saffron whiskers have the makings of a beard. I can't smell my breath, but catching my teeth in the reflection, I *can* smell my breath. I wipe the sweat off my face with the tablecloth and, holding it up, I see the dirt has created a Shroud of Turin. I toss the shroud to the front seat, struggling to unwind.

The protection offered by the SHERP cocoon has only taken me away from my worries for about five minutes. Now my head's back at Pastor Ron's office, bashing on the walls, the anguish of nearly getting Kanye but not quite. And now the torment is taking over.

JUST BECAUSE YOU'RE PARANOID DOESN'T MEAN THEY'RE NOT AFTER YOU

You need to know I have receipts. Goblins in the shadows, out to take me down.

Eleven years ago, on the morning of the release of my first book, *Murder in Mississippi*, a review went up on Amazon:

> Poorly written, lacks depth. This is a terrible book!
> He annoyingly inserts himself into the story's narrative.
> Mr Safran claims that this was his 'Truman Capote' moment, but he is no Truman Capote. This is not a work of literature, and unlike Capote's true crime classic *In Cold Blood*, it lacks substantial depth into the human condition.

The review was authored by 'Hummus Man'.

I was blindsided. Who was this Hummus Man? How had he, within a few hours of the book going on sale, bought it and read it? I clicked about. Hummus Man had also reviewed a hunting knife, and a t-shirt featuring the mascot of a rugby union team from a Queensland university.

Well, well, well, I thought. *Isn't that interesting.*

You know who also went to this Queensland university? A member of my extended family. I had sent an advance copy of the book to this man's wife, so it seemed quite plausible, but maybe I was being paranoid? People tell me I'm paranoid. And I had to admit, the t-shirt review was circumstantial evidence at best. I had to dig deeper.

A tab on the side of the screen took me to Hummus Man's Amazon wishlist. I clicked it, and on this new page, up came the name of that extended family member.

I called the wife of Hummus Man. She could tell I was upset. I asked how would she like it if I tried to sabotage her career?

'Okay, well, look, John. I think this is something you're going to have to talk to him about directly. I hear your concerns.'

'I'm happy to talk to him about it!' I huffed.

'John wants to talk to you,' I heard her say.

'Hang on, what's, what's it about?' came Hummus Man's reply.

'He says you're trashing his book on Amazon.'

'Oh ... well ... um,' he spluttered. He had been caught on the run. He hadn't prepared for this. 'Well ... I don't need to talk to him. John just needs to learn how to take criticism.'

'Hey,' his wife said, returning to the phone, sounding exhausted.

'What, I'm not entitled to an opinion?' Hummus Man said in the background, sulkily.

'Yes, you're entitled to an opinion,' she said.

She told me she would try to talk Hummus Man around.

By the next day, Hummus Man had edited his review of my book. He had added, 'I think it's very important for aspiring authors to maintain a sense of professionalism when dealing with criticism. Some tend to focus way too much on the reviewer, rather than responding directly to the review.'

The day after that, he had added a new review, to go with the one for my book, the hunting knife and the university sports team t-shirt. This one was for *In Cold Blood* by Truman Capote:

> This is a superb read for lovers of true crime. Some authors today try to emulate Capote's writing talent and insightful genius, but they can never match up to the master. It's quite a shame he wasn't able to deal with the criticisms of his later works and later died of alcoholism, drug addiction and poor health.

I'm well on my way to serving myself on a platter to Hummus Man, like a hog with an apple in his mouth, except this hog is doing it to himself.

> Safran fails again! Get this – he has a book about Kanye with no Kanye!
>
> – Hummus Man, Verified Amazon Reviewer

DAY FIVE

It has worked. Knowing I'm safe in the SHERP has granted me the most wonderful of sleeps. I'm revitalised.

I look to the back of the vehicle. How did I not think of this last night? I can lock the SHERP from the inside.

I lock the door and spend the morning typing out hundreds and hundreds of words, more than I have on any other day in the mansion. More than I do back home in my apartment.

Who'd have thought? The perfect writer's retreat is not a homestead by a waterfall in Daylesford. It's a metal box lined with camo, parked on the grounds of a Hitler enthusiast.

By the afternoon, I'm still going. I'm bashing the keys and the words keep flowing and flowing. A million frogs are croaking from the creeks and streams of Calabasas. If you are out there too, crickets, rubbing your wings together, producing the universal sound for 'you're not funny', you're not psyching me out. The frogs are drowning you out. Thank you, frogs. Thank you, God, for sending

DAY FIVE

the frogs. You rained frogs on Egypt, to strike down the Pharaoh and the oppressors of the Jews, and you have sent them once again to strike down my oppressors.

IDENTITY THEFT

So, Kanye secretly visits rabbis, seems to have a reverence for Jewish scripture, enough so that he writes it on his walls, but he thinks Hitler was right. Why can't he just be an antisemitic antisemite – why does he have to be a philosemitic antisemite? Is he repulsed by Jews *because* he's attracted to them? Like a closeted jock who beats up gay people?

After his tweet about going 'death con 3' on Jewish people, he went on to write: 'The funny thing is I actually can't be Anti Semitic because black people are actually Jew'.

And he didn't stop there. He carried on this line of thought in an interview, saying, cryptically – almost impenetrably – that Jews are 'the 12 lost tribes of Judah, the blood of Christ, who the people known as the race Black really are'.

I clocked that this language was the vibe of the Black Hebrew Israelites. It made me wonder – when Kanye says 'Jew' and I say 'Jew', are we even talking about the same thing?

THE BLACK HEBREW ISRAELITE

Standing on a busy street in Harlem, I couldn't spy through the windows of the Black Hebrew Israelites centre. The shopfront windows were painted maroon, emblazoned with Stars of David.

This was interesting. The Black Israelites were accused of being hostile to Jews, but groups like that usually prefer symbols like swastikas. Certainly not the Star of David, unless it was struck through with a red cross.

In white lettering on the glass of the doors were the names of the Twelve Tribes of Israel, from the Torah. But alongside each was the name of a modern-day peoples – the groups that the Black Hebrew Israelites claim are the descendants of the Twelve Tribes of Israel.

> *Judah – The Negroes*
> *Benjamin – West Indians*
> *Levi – Haitian*
> *Simeon – Dominicans*

Zebulon – Guatemala to Panama
Ephraim – Puerto Ricans
Manasseh – Cubans
Gad – North American Indians
Reuben – Seminole Indians
Naphtali – Argentina and Chile
Asher – Colombia to Uruguay
Issachar – Mexicans

A Black man was guarding the door. I approached.

'There's a meeting taking place,' he said.

'I can't come to the meeting, just to hang about?'

'It's a private meeting.'

I asked the guy who the Black Hebrew Israelites were.

'It's an ethno-religious movement, amongst Black and Hispanic and indigenous people.'

That word 'ethno' was the sneaky one. At least for Jews like me.

The conventional view was that Jews like me – 'white' Jews – made up 80 per cent of the world's Jewish population. Jews with roots in Eastern Europe, in countries like Poland and Hungary. Yet no allowance was made for that ethno group in the Black Israelite's list.

It occurred to me that I couldn't enter because, literally, my name was not on the door.

'We are the actual descendants of the ancient Israelites,' he said.

'And that's different to how Jews like me think they're the descendants?'

'Yep.'

So, I was erased.

'So why have I got it wrong?'

'The Bible, Revelations 3:9, tells us somebody is going to be pretending to be Jews who aren't. Somebody is essentially going to steal the identity of the Jews.'

'And that's who I am?'

'Yep.'

Jews don't include Revelations in the Torah, the Old Testament – it's part of the Christians' New Testament. This is confusing, but it isn't my fault: despite the Black Hebrew Israelites believing the bits of the Bible the Jews don't believe in, they see themselves as Jews, not Christian.

I asked the man at the maroon doors what Revelations 3:9 said.

'I will make those who are of the synagogue of Satan, who claim to be Jews though they are not, but are liars – I will make them come and fall down at your feet.'

Damn.

'And do you think that the Jews who think they're the Jews are just innocently mistaken, or is there something kind of intentional going on there?'

'I certainly believe it's something sinister. Maybe not every single one of you in particular, but the concept I believe was very sinisterly concocted.'

'Oh yeah,' I said, my entire Jewish life speeding through my head (bagel to the grave?). 'And why did the Jews concoct it?'

He says by convincing the world we are the Chosen People we get to leverage power. And it also provides a cover story, deflecting from who we really are: the children of Satan.

'And what about some people who put this positive message

out there, where it's like – the Black and the Jewish community in America, they're two minorities. They've been screwed over in the past, and they should work together as brothers?'

He stayed quiet, just eyeballed me.

Things were tense, but I didn't mind. I was hearings things I'd never heard before. He didn't deny that the Holocaust had happened, but he was in a bad mood with the Jews about it. He said the Bible revealed the Jews will suffer a great tragedy. So, if you believe in Bible prophecies, it appeared the Holocaust was that great tragedy. Which would validate that *my* Jews were the real Jews.

But the Holocaust only fed into his agitation. It got in the way of what he believed to be the truth: the great tragedy the Bible foretold was Black people enslaved and taken to America. Validating that *his* Jews were the real Jews.

So it was one or the other. Only one of us would get to walk away a Jew, and it couldn't be more important to both of us standing on that street in Harlem.

His beliefs led to fascinating places. If the Black Hebrew Israelites were the real Jews, given the Torah promised Israel to the Chosen People, which side did he take in the Israel–Palestine conflict?

'We don't believe either of them should be there. We should be there.'

I could see me and the Black Hebrew Israelite had reached an impasse.

'I'm not saying this happens often,' I tried, 'but a few years ago there was an attack in a synagogue where the guy had put Black Hebrew Israelite stuff in his journal?'

He brushed this away as the FBI blowing things out of proportion.

THE ATTACK IN THE SYNAGOGUE

I only missed one turnoff during the hour-long drive from downtown New York. But I shouldn't flatter myself for that achievement. It was five in the morning, so I had the highway pretty much to myself. I could slow to a crawl and think hard at forks in the road.

As I pulled up, a Black man was wheeling a Hasidic Jew in a wheelchair up the street.

It felt refreshing, leaving the skyscrapers behind. Here in Monsey, streetlamps glowed upon rows of willow and pine trees. I spotted a second Hasid, drawing on a cigarette, on the grass outside the synagogue. Its smoke disappeared into the mist that hung over the man's shtreimel, the distinctive hat – the wheel of fur – found atop a Hasid.

'Saffron, the most expensive spice,' the Hasid mused when I introduced myself.

I fumbled out that I had come here because of 'what happened ... the tragedy'.

The Hasid took a slow draw of his cigarette, sizing up this outsider.

'This is the house.' He pointed his cigarette across the tiny car park. 'This is the house that got attacked.'

The house, like the synagogue – like most homes in Monsey – was Dutch Colonial. Weatherboard monsters with farmhouse roofs.

The house in question belonged to the Rebbe, the highest-ranking rabbi in a Hasidic community.

In late December 2019, Rebbe Chaim Rottenberg hosted a party. Around 140 people squeezed inside as he lit the candles of the big silver menorah, honouring the seventh night of Hanukkah.

'So, the guy walked in, he closed the door,' the Hasid began. 'And he had a big machete.'

Machete. I felt the word.

'There was a man who was marrying off his son the following week, and he was there with his son. And he was the first one that the guy swung at. The guy swiped down, he cut the front of his shtreimel. So, people started throwing a coat rack at the guy.'

Some fled out the back door, down the porch stairs. One older man, seventy-something, held his ground.

'He just had open-heart surgery a few months before.' The old man ambled towards the intruder. 'The guy almost cut his arm off on the first swipe.'

The old man backed away, but two others stayed.

'There were two men that were both a little soft in the head, you know? And they were like, "Stop it! Stop it!" And he kept chasing them around with the machete. He lopped his ear, his ear was almost taken off. And the other guy, he had defensive wounds on his arm.

THE ATTACK IN THE SYNAGOGUE

Just saw him yesterday, I gave him twenty dollars. Soft in the head, that's how you'd describe him.'

I glanced at the Hasid's hands; the glow of ash was running out of cigarette to burn.

'The guy got a cut on his head,' he went on. 'At least the shtreimel protected him. I mean, one of the other guys was murdered.'

Later, law enforcement raided the home of the machete-wielder, a Black man, Grafton Thomas. They found a journal with references to 'Adolf Hitler', 'Nazi Culture' and 'Hebrew Israelites', drawings of a Star of David and a swastika, and use of the obscure term 'ebinoid Israelite'. An FBI agent told the court this term 'appears to be a reference to the "Black Hebrew Israelite" movement, in which groups of African-Americans assert that they are the descendants of the ancient Israelites'.

The Hasid, finishing his cigarette, invited me into the synagogue, handing me tefillin to wrap around my arm and head. I stayed for the morning prayer service, then crossed the small car park to the Rebbe's house. His study was lined wall to wall with bookshelves; you know there are a lot of books when you can smell that there are books before you even get into the room. These were leather-bound, with gold Hebrew lettering on the spines.

Hasidic men typically wear a black woollen robe over their suit, tied at the waist with a sash. Rebbe Rottenberg's robe was a cut above that: chocolate-brown wool, patterned with copper-coloured leaves and flowers. He was crowned with a hoiche, a high black felt hat with a brim. His peyot, the sidelocks that dangle from a Hasid's head, were like a pair of those long, cream wafer sticks, ringed with chocolate swirls.

His long beard, snow white, was easily the brightest colour in this room. His chair was upholstered in plumb-red velvet and seemingly everything else was lacquered brown, the lights throwing a soft golden glow across the Rebbe.

Within Hasidism there are different sects – dynasties that roll back hundreds of years. Rebbe Rottenberg's dynasty is known as Koson, after the village in Ukraine where his sect was founded.

'You're writing about antisemitism?' he asked. 'What are you writing?'

'Okay, so —' I began.

'There is antisemitism,' the Rebbe cut in. 'There always was. And it's here to stay. So, what's more to write than these two sentences?'

'Oh, yeah. Well, no, that's a good point,' I said, almost sure it wasn't. 'But there's this famous Black American entertainer called Kanye West and he said he loved Adolf Hitler and —'

'Many people said that,' he cut in. 'What are we going to do? A goy hates a Jew. He doesn't hate you less than me. So it has nothing to do with our dress code. It has nothing to do with keeping Shabbos or not. It's being a Jew. Why?'

I knew he was going to cut me off again, so I kept my mouth shut. But the silence became too much, so I ventured to answer.

'Well, I guess —'

'Because when the Torah was given to us, Hashem brought down hate, for the goyim to hate a Jew.'

He was saying this: in the days of old, Moses stood atop a mountain. And God – Hashem – gave him the Torah, to give to the Jews. This was the most blessed moment for the Jews. But at the same time, he put a hatred for Jews in the hearts of non-Jews, the goyim. However, the Rebbe went on to explain, Hashem didn't always activate hatred of Jews in the hearts of goyim. Often it lay dormant.

'It is controlled according to our behaviour. Why did He do this? Very simple. The Torah requests of us to distance ourselves from the goyim. If we keep that distance, they will never harm us.'

He held a view that I hadn't come across before. According to him, forcing Jews into ghettos, as so many regimes had over the course of history, was good for the Jews.

'The ghettos – those days were fine. The trouble always started when we broke out of the ghettos, got involved.'

He homes in on the early years of the Nazis, when they were just getting started. They forced Jews to adopt a second name on their identity papers – 'Israel' if they were male, 'Sarah' if they were female – so they couldn't blend into non-Jewish society. For Rebbe Rottenberg, this was terrific. As was another Nazi proclamation.

'In 1933, they stopped the Jewish students from walking into the academies, into the colleges. Why? Because we don't belong there. Do you get it?'

I had a go. 'They stopped us, but don't blame the Nazis – that was Hashem working through the Nazis?'

'That's what I'm saying. Hashem wants the distance. We don't belong to be with them. And if we don't keep that distance, they will keep the distance for us. You got that point?'

My mind was in flux, taking this in.

'Wake up to reality,' he pleaded, with a clap.

'It's an interesting way to look at it. That God is working through these antisemites to teach us to stay separate. And —'

'It's not interesting. It's a fact. Look, where did World War II start? Where did that ruler, that devil grow up?'

The Rebbe laid it out. The Reform Jewish movement, founded in Germany in the mid-nineteenth century, tossed aside strict religious practices, endeavouring to blend in with their non-Jewish neighbours. This angered Hashem, so he sent in Adolf Hitler and the Nazis to remind the Jews in that part of the world to stick to their own. And serve as a larger lesson to Jews across the world.

'Reform Jews are to blame for the Holocaust?' I asked.

'No one in the secular world wants to admit, wants to see it that way. But I'm telling you true facts.'

I was not desensitised to this line of thinking. The Holocaust was Hashem's grace, the God of Moses working through SS and Gestapo soldiers to steer us back to the righteous path.

My conversation with the Rebbe moved on to Hanukkah 2019, the night a man burst into his house wielding a machete. It was disorienting – I could peer out the open door of his study to the next room, where in one online news story I'd seen the blood smeared on the floor.

What had been reported in the media as a tragedy, the Rebbe saw differently.

'I thank God. There were so many miracles in this one story, so many visible miracles.'

'What miracles?'

'There were about 140 human beings in this home before he came in. And thank God, no one was killed. And —'

Now it was my turn to interrupt. 'But didn't a man die?'

'One man. Three months later.'

Without a pause, he rolled on, but I will fill you in. Joseph Neumann, seventy-two, suffered a slice wound through the neck, a shattered arm and a fractured skull – the machete penetrating his brain. He fell into a coma, and succumbed to his injuries three months later.

Back to the miracles.

'All others he touched, he slashed the clothing to the body. Only skin is scratched, the body didn't go down. He slashed hats through to the skull, skull only need get a couple of stitches.'

The miracles kept coming.

'Had he walked in five minutes earlier, God forbid, or three minutes later, it would be such a disaster. Why? Five minutes earlier, we were still in the middle of the Hanukkah ceremony. Everybody was focused to one direction, with their back to the door. Three minutes later, this would be when the men had left – forty women in the house alone. So, Hashem, he made the minutes when it happened to be so exact . . . It's unbelievable.'

I proposed a hypothetical: would he feel differently if someone in his family had been among the victims that night? My attempted gotcha didn't work. Three out of the four surviving victims were his sons.

A young man, wrapped in tefillin, hovered at the open door to the Rebbe's study.

'Here's one of them.' He beamed. 'Here's one of my children that was slashed.'

'Oh, really?'

'Yes,' the son said.

'I'm really sorry to hear that.' I didn't know what to say. 'How big was the knife?'

'A big knife.'

'What message did you take from it?'

'Live like a Jew is supposed to live.' The son pointed at the tefillin wrapped on his arm.

'Put on tefillin every day?' I asked. 'Fair enough.'

THE EEL

Two days later, I had flown back from New York to Los Angeles. The man outside the maroon doors in Harlem had made his mark. He was still wisping around my head when I was digging into Italian takeaway at the kitchen table of Matt Stone, co-creator of *South Park*. I knew he had grappled with the question I was facing.

'So what's up with your episode of *South Park* with Cupid Ye? What was the origin story of doing that?'

'I was talking to a Black friend of mine when the Kanye stuff was all going down,' said Matt, who is Jewish. 'And, somehow, I got around to explaining the Black Hebrew Israelites and who they were. They're always out on Venice Beach.' He gestured through the wall of his house, towards the famous LA beach.

In his work, Matt had poked fun at the Mormon church for their dubious historical claims. Most atheist historians agreed that a figure corresponding to Jesus existed in the Middle East, they just didn't think he performed miracles. In contrast, these historians didn't think Jesus came to America, as the Mormons proposed. Matt thought the historical claims of the Black Hebrew Israelites on Venice Beach fell short too.

'I read up about them and their goofy beliefs, and one of their goofy beliefs is that the real Jews are Black. That Black Americans are the Lost Tribes of Israel, the real Chosen People.'

When Matt explained that to his Black friend, he didn't respond as Matt had expected.

'I saw this little look in my friend's eyes. Just a totally natural reaction to being told that you, in fact, are the Chosen People. It's a pretty enticing thought. I just saw this moment from him of, like, "Oh, well. That's nice." And it is, for a group that has never been able to really feel that way in America.'

He took me through the brainstorming and spitballing that took place in the *South Park* writers' room.

'So we started from a place of trying to just put Kyle, our little Jewish kid, and Tolkien (née Token), our little Black kid, in the situation where somebody's going to be pulling them apart – someone's going to be aggravating that relationship. And then of course we just started thinking, well, of course Eric Cartman would be the person to do that.'

In the episode, Kyle and Tolkien had become creative collaborators, producing TikToks together. Cartman, indoctrinated by an angel inspired by Kanye, endeavours to tear them apart. The angel, named 'Cupid Ye', whispers Black Hebrew Israelite talking points in Tolkien's ears.

'It doesn't take a lot to poke people – to poke these two populations and then have them get mad at each other. And it doesn't really seem there's a winning strategy for either one of those groups. Who's winning by making those two groups not like each other?'

On occasion I'd heard progressive folks pitch that white Christians were the puppetmasters, stirring up trouble between Black and Jewish people to maintain power. But that made me uncomfortable, hitting my ears as the same kind of conspiratorial thinking as Jews being the puppetmasters.

Still, Kanye trashing the Jews could be a confidence booster for him. Enough Americans had told Black people they were lousy humans. Taking the mantle of The Chosen, as Kanye had – 'Black people are actually Jew' – would be pretty appealing after centuries of slavery followed by Jim Crow.

But for Kanye to travel down this path, he needed to label Jews (my Jews) as lousy humans. To take back the mantle of The Chosen People, it had to have been stolen in the first place; for this story to add up, he needed to build an alternative world in his head by means of cherrypicking and hyperbole.

A case study: his nemesis, the chairman and CEO of JP Morgan Chase, was Christian. But despite his fury towards this man, Kanye didn't deliberate over the corrupted essence of the Christian. Rather, to feed the beast in his head, he simply recast this Christian as a Jew.

I had been wondering why a man so invested in dissing the Jews was drawn to Judaism. This combustible mix would explain it. Kanye loved the story of the Jews as the Chosen People, and he wanted in. But to get in – to become the hero of that story – the Jews needed to get out.

That theory wasn't a watertight answer to my question, but maybe it was as close to an answer a question as slippery as an eel can have.

Sucking in another string of pasta from the takeaway box in Matt's kitchen, I asked about his Black wife's response to the Cupid Ye episode. 'When she saw the episode, did she cry and, in tears, go, "Oh, you understand me!"'

'No, my wife doesn't even watch the show,' said Matt. 'So I'm the one that cries.'

PEOPLE OF TRAUMA

I hope I'm not giving you the wrong impression. There are Black Americans who are 'regular' Jews. Shen Hrobowski was a Black American who converted to Judaism. A while ago, when she was living in Melbourne, she emailed me about her conversion, but this was the first time we were catching up, at an LA café. I was telling her about visiting Kanye's secret rabbi and how we all just blabbed and blabbed and put on tefillin, the black-hatters and me, the secular Jew, in my Yemulke.

'And that's what I love. That's why I joined the nation,' said Shen. 'I converted at the Orthodox level, but I don't cover my hair. I'm wearing a Tupac shirt, I've got on slacks. I'm just chilling. I'm just my authentic self. I feel like I can be. And I'm Black first and then I'm Jewish. So I kind of just roll with who I am.'

I forgot to write down questions ahead of our chat. But luckily I'm good at light small talk.

'And did your ancestors come over from Africa as slaves, or did they come in the later stage?'

'Yes,' she said. As in, yes, they came to America on slave ships.

Shen became curious about Judaism because people kept asking about her last name, Hrobowski.

'"What is that name? Are you Jewish?" As Black Americans, we don't really know where our surnames come from. Maybe I'm Polish. Maybe my ancestors could have been Jewish? But there's a chance that it could be a slave name.'

'That's really heavy,' I said. 'They could have been Jewish slave owners.'

This threw her a little. 'That's interesting. I don't imagine that. But I have no idea.'

(Some radical Black American groups, like Nation of Islam, say Jews were behind the transatlantic slave trade. Most historians say everyone from Berbers to Arabs to Dutch to Swedes took part. In the American South in the 1830s, out of the 12,000 major slave holders (fifty slaves or more), twenty were Jewish, or 0.16 per cent. The overall Jewish population in the American South at the time was between 1 and 3 per cent.)

Shen was right. Because of slavery, the history of Black American families can be hard to trace. Later, the only document I could find pointing to the religion of the Hrobowskis suggested they were Christian: a baptism announcement.

'All that trauma kind of shapes you, even though it didn't happen to me,' Shen said. 'All this stuff gets passed down and passed down and passed down. And now I've become a Black Jew as a result of looking for a home. My family's like, "What are you doing? Why are you going through this?" It just feels like home.'

This is where the story gets a little bumpy.

'There's bad apples everywhere,' Shen said. 'My Jewish mother-in-law – she tried to stop the marriage. She flew out with her sister. They tag-teamed me in a Starbucks. They're twins. They tag-teamed me and they said, "You guys shouldn't get married."'

Shen's mother-in-law's issue was twofold. Not only was Shen Black, she was a convert. 'She said, "Black people need to sit with Black people. And converts need to sit with converts."'

I whistled, taken aback. The Jewish mother-in-law was a 'brown' Moroccan, by the way. I couldn't figure out how that fitted into the big picture. My mind was already overspilling, taking in what the mother-in-law had said.

'And my rabbi told her, "Shen is just as much Jewish as my daughter, so don't ever come over here like that." So she apologised. It was really, really tough. Fast-forward seven years, she loves her grandkids and it's almost like it never happened.'

I told her synagogues in my area had beefed up security in response to threats, putting armed guards at the gate, and that some people had turned this against the Jews. Their argument being that Black Jews would feel intimidated seeing men with guns, because they would have been targeted by law enforcement over the course of their lives.

I can't always articulate what's in my head with eloquence, so I wasn't surprised Shen could barely follow what I was getting at.

'You mean, do we mind that there's security and stuff? No.'

I had another go.

'Do you have a bee in your bonnet? Because Jews, they'll say, oh, we're a minority, like Black people are. And then people will say, nah, stop with that, Jews. You've become white people. You get to walk through the streets as white people. So knock it off.'

'Honestly, we use the phrase "people of colour" here in the USA. I'm going to start changing it to "people of trauma" to make sure I include Jews. Because I do think, yes, Jews are people of trauma. That's it. You can't just blend in. So that's my perspective.'

She poured another cup of tea from the pot.

'I remember seeing you on the street when I was living in Melbourne. It was so weird. And I remember watching your stuff, it was – man, I like him. He's nuts, but I like his style. He just kind of puts himself out there. So I feel like you were part of my journey, as well as a lot of other Jews that I've met, people who were their authentic selves. I've thought, I'm going to meet this dude one day.'

I'M GOING TO MEET THIS DUDE ONE DAY, PROFESSOR GRIFF

'You were in the wrong borough.' Public Enemy's Professor Griff laughed. 'You were in Brooklyn. Long Island is out that way. And I was in Westbury.'

Yes, I had turned up to the wrong Schneck Avenue. And Professor Griff had a plane to catch. So we were now meeting up at LaGuardia Airport. Airy and clean, with trees that looked like they should be outdoors, indoors. Pretty nice as far as airports go.

Professor Griff was a rapper and 'Minister for Information' in Public Enemy. In high school, on my shelf I had their cassette slid in between Beastie Boys and LL Cool J. Professor Griff was my ground zero – the first person to alert me to the fact that there was beef between Black and Jewish Americans, through Public Enemy's music, but also stories and interviews in magazines. When it came to the Jews, he was Kanye before there was Kanye.

When I met him at LaGuardia, Professor Griff wore a back-to-front baseball cap, a black turtleneck and a chain. So roughly still the same guy that had looked out at me from magazines when I was a teenager.

I began by bringing up Public Enemy's early years, the late eighties.

'When was there the first bit of friction? That, hang on, we're saying these things in our lyrics that are controversial and people are going to push back?'

I see his guard go up. Despite my effort to not raise any alarms, he can tell this is rolling towards the matter of Public Enemy and the Jews.

'Public Enemy came from a long history, a long legacy of revolutionary activists and revolutionary spoken-word artists. Revolutionary period. Especially in music. So that didn't just happen. There's always been those revolutionaries, whether they recorded or not. Black preachers in the church. Even in the streets, especially during the revolutionary sixties. And then when we started, when we were allowed to have control over our own recordings, some of us put it in the recordings.'

He pulled out vinyl records from his tote bag. He had been crate digging in second-hand record stores that day. One was a spoken-word record from Martin Luther King; another, by civil rights activist WEB Du Bois.

'You can still find the stuff on wax, but you have to know where to look. So it's not new. So when you talk about the friction – the friction didn't start with Public Enemy. The friction was way before.'

I feel a little friction now.

He said Prince told him, before he died, that music was losing its revolutionary zeal.

'He said music today is like bubblegum. You buy it cheap, chew the taste out of it, spit it out, and hope you don't get it on your shoe.'

'So what happened? You were asked to leave Public Enemy or —'

'No, I was never asked to leave.'

Did I have it wrong? 'Because when I was a teenager and I was reading the articles in the magazines, it was like, you said something too inflammatory about Jewish people, and that's the reason why they kicked you out.'

In 1989, the *Washington Times* quoted Griff as saying 'the Jews finance these experiments on AIDS with black people', that they were responsible for 'the majority of the wickedness that goes on across the globe', and dared Jews to send 'their faggot little hit men' after him.

Professor Griff said he had a cassette recording of that interview conducted by the *Washington Times*, but it was lost in a house fire. He believed this cassette would have vindicated him. I couldn't figure out if he was saying he never spoke those spicy words, or that there was a context that ameliorated their spice.

'So my cassette is gone. And then when I get a chance to sit down and defend myself, I'm never believed. It's like, what do I have to lie about? I'm sixty-two years old. You destroyed everything that I built.'

'How did people destroy what you built?'

'House burnt down. Shot at. Poisoned.'

Woah. I'd never heard these claims before.

'But by who?'

'I don't know. You have to tell me.'

I felt the marble begin its roll, on its way to you-know-who.

'Are you suggesting Jewish people tried to poison you? They're the ones that burnt down your house?'

'No, I wouldn't. Even in interviews like this, I never even mentioned the term. I never say who it is.'

I was confused. Because it was true – he never mentioned 'the term'. But I know that he knows that I know what's up.

'A name I learnt for the first time, listening to Public Enemy, was Louie Farrakhan.' I began to lightly rap. *'Louie Farrakhan's a prophet who you have to listen to —'*

'It's not Louie, it's Louis.' (Fact check: I flubbed the line.)

Louis Farrakhan headed up the Nation of Islam. Its beliefs differed from those of the Black Hebrew Israelites, but there was an overlapping theme: Black Americans who considered Jews to be at the centre of their woes.

'I think all of us in Public Enemy were studying who we are. And that's part of who we are. Understanding that particular body of work.'

'And are you now part of the Nation of Islam?'

He answered my question with a question, 'You ever watch porn?'

'Yes.'

'Then are you a porn-star artist? See what I mean?'

He meant that just because you look into something, it doesn't mean you're all-in.

'Fair enough. That's a good point.'

Professor Griff wanted to underscore his case.

'I've studied James Baldwin,' he said of the Black, gay author and civil rights activist. 'I did a lecture and I had a James Baldwin quote and a picture of James Baldwin. Somebody asked me was

I homosexual, because I showed James Baldwin. I'm like, yeah, no, I don't play those kinds of childish games, man.'

I recalled a Public Enemy show in Melbourne in the nineties. Flavor Flav, the group's hype man, who sported a giant clock around his neck, started spouting off.

'We heard you have a politician down here called Pauline Hanson and she a nasty motherfucker.'

The crowd went crazy, cheering on Flavor Flav.

'We heard she a bitch.'

Some concert-goers weren't entirely happy with the term 'bitch', but overall the crowd let it slide.

Flavor Flav went on to outline the various ways he would fornicate with the senator for Queensland, crowd enthusiasm waning along the way as they mentally punched 'Feminism' versus 'Black Empowerment' into their intersectionality calculators.

Griff's quotes in the *Washington Times* couldn't have been clearer. In contrast, Public Enemy's lyrical references to Jews were opaque, like: 'Crucifixion ain't no fiction/ So called Chosen frozen.'

'To us, it wasn't even that serious then,' Griff told me when I brought up those lyrics. 'We was young, in our twenties.'

When our conversation moved from Public Enemy to Kanye West, he opened up more. He felt old-school rappers like him could provide guidance to artists like Kanye.

'I think that Kanye West thing is spiralling out of control. The older guys have went through certain things and we've made amends, we've apologised for certain things. We've humbled ourselves. We've tried to right certain wrongs. But those artists refuse to sit down with us.'

Professor Griff said he has reached out to younger artists but been rebuffed.

'They say, "You're old school, so why do we need to sit down with you?" I say, wow. Well, we have a history and some experience that we need to pass down to you. That you won't make certain mistakes and say certain things. Because these certain things I heard Kanye say? I thought we've crossed those bridges before. So we got to go back across the bridge and burn it down again? No sir. No! You grow. You understand what I'm saying? You grow up.'

The conversation had felt a little uncomfortable at times. But ultimately, to me, this was a feel-good story. The man who in 1989 blamed Jews 'for the majority of wickedness in the world' was now telling Kanye to knock it off with the antisemitism.

I told him what else Kanye had been up to.

'He makes all his employees and contractors wear black from head to toe. The guy at the cement mixer has to wear black.'

The cultural divide evaporated. He dropped his voice.

'You think he's trying to channel a certain energy?'

'I don't know. I guess.'

'Well, if you're dealing with occult magic – black and white magic – and you're diving into that realm, what are you doing? Having everyone wear black? It's not a goddamn fashion statement.'

I sparked up. I couldn't believe my luck. Meeting a childhood hero, who, unexpectedly, wanted to discuss the occult.

'It's like, Kanye, what are you doing?' he said. 'So maybe he's operating in – dipping and dabbling – in realms, worlds. Some people go through those doors and never come back.'

'Well, he's definitely attracted to the flame of pushing buttons and going into dangerous areas, which can obviously be creatively interesting.'

'Well, I think if you're not really careful, it can destroy you as an individual. You can be a walking zombie. You can be the physical person, but inside's destroyed. You understand what I'm saying?'

He leant in.

'Those demonic and satanic, Luciferian forces. It's nothing to play with, man. It's really nothing to play with. And we have to be mindful and careful.'

KANYE, THE NAZIS AND THE OCCULT

To the mainstream, Kanye's invocation of Nazism was dangerous on a political level. But not everyone who feared Nazism limited it to this realm. One book on my bookshelf back in Melbourne was *The Nazis and the Occult: The dark forces unleashed by the Third Reich* by Paul Roland.

Some feared that dabbling in Nazism was like dabbling in witchcraft – you were in danger of releasing otherworldly forces. So I wasn't surprised that Kanye's 'meltdown' was being interpreted by Professor Griff through a mystical lens.

The narrative people built around Kanye was that he was a man of Christ. But after I returned to Australia, a counter-narrative congealed. He might have turned – was now a man of the Antichrist. Kanye would proudly pose for photos wearing a t-shirt of black metal artist Burzum, aka Varg Vikernes. That is, his music was black metal, not black as in Black American.

Varg Vikernes was a white Norwegian, and a pagan who openly

opposed Christ. And he went all-in. In the early nineties he burned down three churches in Norway. But if that wasn't enough, at around the same time, he murdered a fellow black metal musician, Øystein Aarseth, who went by the stage name Euronymous. He was found dead in a stairwell with twenty-three stab wounds, two to the head, five to the neck and sixteen to the back.

So Burzum wasn't the same as other metal acts, like Iron Maiden or Slayer. You didn't inadvertently pull on a Burzum t-shirt. Which was why Christians, who celebrated Kanye when he was proclaiming his love for Jesus, would be alarmed to find a smiling Kanye promoting Burzum, sampling his music and featuring footage of a burning church in a music video.

But Kanye only did all that after I'd left America and was back in my homeland. While I was there, people like Professor Griff were only sensing that Kanye, the man of Jesus, might be reversing course.

Another who could detect a change in things was Bryson Gray, a Black American rapper and a Christian. He had worked with Kanye but was now hinting online that he had concerns about him. I punched Bryson's number into my phone. I was in Los Angeles and he in Tennessee. He began by telling me how he had ended up working with Kanye.

'Kanye reached out to me. Not him personally, of course. It was his right-hand man. He said Kanye wanted me to come out there to help work on some songs.'

Bryson was sceptical.

'I thought it was fake at first, because who reaches out to somebody, with something that important, on Instagram? I guess we are in the new world. But long story short, it ended up not being fake.'

Why did Kanye seek him out?

'Kanye wanted me to make sure everything he sang was aligned with Christianity, and help write also.'

Bryson was a 'Kanye West fanatic' growing up. Kanye caught Bryson's attention when, in 2019, he released his ninth studio album, *Jesus Is King*, and started hosting Sunday Services at his mansion. Yes, my mansion. The services held in the UFO.

'At first, I didn't know if Kanye was legitimate or not in embracing Jesus. But then I started believing it. Although sometimes I didn't, if you know what I mean.'

Kanye's people sent Bryson an airline ticket and he boarded a plane to Japan. 'It was my first time out of the country, so Tokyo was strange. But it was fifteen people working. I actually thought it was fun, because I've never worked on music with that large a group of people. So it's chaotic, but fun in a way.'

He had to pinch himself. He was in a recording studio in Tokyo, laying down tracks with Kanye West. Following this dizzying experience, he returned to Tennessee. Kanye didn't end up releasing any songs that Bryson had worked on, but he wasn't too fazed. He filed that under 'it happens'.

Then Bryson started hearing stories about Kanye. Like Professor Griff, he felt something was off.

'I don't know what's going on with Kanye. When I was with him, he seemed to be on fire for Christ. We talked about the Bible. We talked about repentance. He liked the fact that I was so biblical. I can't explain to you this new Kanye. I don't understand. But a lot of times when you fall away from Christ, you do a freefall. And, unfortunately, it seems like he's freefalling. He isn't old, but he's in his forties, and you never know what could happen next. On Judgement Day he will be judged by what he's doing. He's in desperate need of repentance, and I hope it happens because he's very influential and powerful. It is good if you have good people around you, and godly people around you. Clearly it's bad if the people you're listening to are all demons. And it irritates me that I must burn a bridge to call it out. But that's what I do. All sin and all wickedness gets called out by me.'

DAY SIX: THE WICKEDNESS

I came to live in a mansion, like Kanye, but I'm living in a car, like Mark. I'm losing my sense of time. Have I taken two or three naps today? For how long? Through the SHERP's windows, morning looks like afternoon looks like dusk.

From my vantage point, lying on the floor of the cabin, a piece of white plastic flapping from a scaffolding pole looks to be a surrender flag.

I'm too drained to leave the vehicle for a power outlet in the mansion, so my laptop lies dead and I'm writing with a pen on my yellow notepad. Food is fine – I have jerky and granola bars – and five sake bottles filled with water, one filled with sake.

I drift into the land of nod once more. In my dream, a red-haired woman in a nice car is slowly crawling through an underground car park. In a snap, the car accelerates to top speed, smashing into a wall.

Jolted awake, I spring up to a sitting position. I feel unsettled. I *know* that car park, but I can't place it.

Yes, I can. It's the one underneath the hospital where my cardiologist practises.

The other shoe drops.

I have seven pills I need to take each day for my heart. I haven't taken them for the last six days.

And the pills are not here. The boxes containing those pills are packed in a suitcase in the hotel where Antoinette is staying.

I turn the handle on the rear of the SHERP and jump out, run across the front grounds and escape to the mansion, into the wormhole, through the big blue room and to the industrial kitchen. My bare feet feel, but need to ignore, the changing surfaces – the rough concrete of the grounds, the moist foam of the blue room, the stinging cold epoxy flooring of the kitchen.

I drop to my knees before one of the sinks and pull open the cabinet doors beneath. I start rummaging through the rubbish bin for Egg McMuffin wrappers. I find one free of Antoinette's scribble. I jump up and lay the wrapper, white side up, on a silver bench. I smooth it out, pull a pen from my pocket, and scrawl *PILLS!* in big letters, then outline which suitcase in the hotel I think they're in.

Darting back out the wormhole, I scan the place for a rock – a heavy but palm-sized rock. I can't immediately see anything that fits the bill. How is this place rockless? The woods behind the mansion must have a rock. I rush across the front grounds towards the two-storey house, deciding I'll circle around behind the buildings this way. But before I reach the two-storey house, I slide to a stop in front of the open garage, where the SHERP is parked. I catch a notion there'll be something in the garage, a substitute, to serve the function of a palm-sized rock.

Sparkling new tools surround me, hanging on the walls. The head of one of the hammers would work if it wasn't attached to the rest of the hammer. I scan screwdrivers, spanners, drills, saws, a crowbar, an axe, shovels, hedge cutters, spirit levels and pliers. But my prayers are answered not by the scores of tools on the wall, but by an item lying atop a toolbox in the corner. A metal tape measure. I grab it, wrap it in the Egg McMuffin wrapper, speed back out the garage, cross the bridge and arrive at the matte black gate that separates me from the street.

With an underarm throw, I lob the Egg McMuffin tape measure over the gate. Thud. I'd have to be pretty unlucky for a neighbour or an imp to have seen that.

DEMON IN THE ATTIC

How many days can I go without my seven pills? I had to start taking them in the first place because of what the cardiologist described as miniature heart attacks.

I had brushed off the pain in my heart, thinking it was no biggie. My back began hurting when I went jogging, which I attributed to the jarring effect of pounding my feet on the ground. Then I figured that the nerves in my back were connected to nerves elsewhere, so the pain in the vicinity of my chest could be alleviated by getting better jogging shoes. It turned out it could only be alleviated by a stent in my artery and seven pills a day.

By now my bare feet are numb, which takes my mind away from the matter of the pills. Crossing back over the bridge, my mind drifts further. As I noticed on my first morning here, along the rooftop of the mansion are what look to be three attics – three triangles, a window in each. I now know two of these are decorative, as I've seen them from inside the mansion: one was in the kitchen, the other above the entrance of the mansion, where the wormhole began. But there is a third window.

I head into the white wormhole, but instead of turning left into the big blue room, I continue up and turn right, into the blue hallway. Making my way up, blue rooms running off either side, I pass by the room with the dresser, where Kanye West's credit card leapt out at me, and the foam-padded recording studio, where a nice skylight brightens the space.

I reach the final blue room on my right, where that third window should be. Inside the room an empty bookshelf is lying on its side, a clear plastic tub filled with electrical cables resting on top and a rolled-up rug leaning against it.

I wander in and look up. There's an attic door, but it's out of reach. Quite the brain teaser. I need a ladder.

Two thoughts drift about my head. First, can I prop that bookshelf up against one of the walls and ... no. In the garage, before, I can't specifically recall spotting a ladder, but how could there not have been one – there were four types of spirit levels. Oh! The office desk in the big blue room, if I placed a chair on that I could ... no. I commit to retrieving a ladder from the garage. Turning around to make my way out the door, I catch it from the corner of my eye: a long pole with a hook, lying flat against the skirting board.

I crouch and grip it in my cold hands. Standing up, bringing the pole to a vertical position, gravity plays its wicked little games. I try to catch the hook into the metal ring on the ceiling, but it's a challenge on my biceps just keeping the pole upright. I bring the hook closer and closer, a delicate dance of hand–eye coordination.

And what a workout! I need to activate my core, I'm feeling it in my arms, shoulders, wrists and legs.

I stumble backwards and crash to earth. Looking up, I've left a white scar in the ceiling, a long one, where the pole has scratched through the blue paint.

Propping myself up, I stand and steady myself. I concentrate, biding my time, biting my tongue. Feeling this is the moment, I hoist up the pole and this time catch the ring on the ceiling. I pull down and the attic door unfolds.

The door is now tilted downwards, revealing a folded-up wooden ladder. I hook the lower rung with the pole and it unfolds in a concertina, the bottom two-thirds clicking into place. I return the pole to where I found it by the skirting board and make my way up.

As I get closer to the opening in the ceiling, I'm unnerved. I stop. Am I making myself vulnerable here? I steel myself and poke my head through the threshold into the unknown.

The attic is not blue. Mildew, rot and decay are having their way with the unpainted wooden walls, floors, ceiling and beams. Light does flood in from the window, but it also creeps in from an opening where shingles from one side of the roof have collapsed into the space.

However, this opening doesn't seem to be letting in any fresh air. Twenty seconds, four dry retches; there's hardened animal faeces and unknown globs. I'm guessing mummified mice or something like that.

None of this, however, is the main event. Staring at me from the corner is a giant bird. A dead and bloodied rodent lies before it.

I'm first thinking it's an eagle. But is it actually a vulture? I can't make sense of it. It doesn't have the noble visage of an eagle, nor the familiar facial features of a vulture. Rather, its head looks to be chopped off from a turkey and placed upon whatever this is.

It returns to its rodent.

I look to the collapsed pile of shingles on the floor, then the hole in the roof from where they fell. That must be how the bird got in. It's keeping to itself, occupied with its meal.

Preparing for the stench, I pull myself into the attic, and find I can stand without needing to duck my head. I make my way to the window, my t-shirt pulled up above my nose. I glance at the bird; it doesn't glance back.

The glass in the window is grimier than it looked to be from the ladder. I squint through it. As the hill across the road comes into focus, from behind me comes a cry – a bloodcurdling cry the likes of which I've never heard before.

Just as I couldn't make sense of the head of a turkey on the body of a vulture, I can't make sense of this cry. It's a quick scrape of a shovel on concrete, running into a quick creak of an unoiled hinge on a gate, finishing on a low, low hiss.

I turn around. The bird is staring right at me, its wings fully spread. Its wingspan is one John Safran, if I was lying on my side. The bird's feathers looked to be black before, when it was feasting on the rodent with its wings tucked in, but stretched out, hit by light from the window, I now see they're dark brown. Its brown talons scratch the floor of the attic, its pink fleshy head shakes. And if there was any doubt regarding what I heard before, that cry fills the room again.

Scrape on concrete, gate creak, low hiss.

Scrape on concrete, gate creak, low hiss.

My nerves are shot. Then it registers that this isn't the worst of it. The bird is blocking me from the ladder to the room below, my exit from this attic.

I turn away from the bird. The window looks like it slides up, but the latches on the windowsill are locked shut. My fingers can't get a hold, slipping off no matter how I approach the latches. I start ramming them with the palms of my hands. They're either painted shut or rusted shut or both.

The bird still crying, I survey the room and look up to the hole in the roof. I give the latches three more punches, but they won't budge.

I boost myself up on the windowsill, gripping the sides of the window frame for balance. I somehow get the notion that this attic is Kanye West's head – that I've found hidden disorder, but now I'm trapped by it.

On my tippy-toes, poking my head through the hole in the roof, I taste freedom. I grip the shingles surrounding the hole and try to pull myself up, tearing my t-shirt, scraping the skin on my forearms, my back and my belly.

I make it about halfway out, but my arms can't take the strain. I return myself to the windowsill.

I look down to the bird, my heavy breathing no match for its cry. This is the motivation I needed. Scraping off more flesh, I manage to pull myself all the way through the hole.

I have to focus, this is too dangerous. (But now I have another notion: Kanye slapping his head, a Tom Thumb version of me crawling out his ear.) Focus!

Now crouching on the slope of the roof, stabilising myself, I peer back down through the hole, at the smashed shingles on the floor of the attic. I realise any other spot on the mansion's roof would be a safer bet than where I am.

I crawl up the slope of the attic roof until I reach the roof of the mansion proper. I now ascend *this* slope, gripping shingles, my hands as numb as my feet.

I reach the apex, the peak of the mansion. Finding my equilibrium, I sit on the ridge of the roof, where the slope running up from the front of the mansion meets the slope running down towards the woods.

As I was climbing through the hole, dusk was taking over, and now darkness has taken over that. I cuddle myself in the cold.

THE HUNCHBACK ON THE ROOF

Years ago, when I gave that hunchback a lift, I was introduced to the idea of synchronicity, and from then on, whenever I crossed paths with a psychic, dream reader or fortune teller, I would ask what that encounter meant. But it took an interview with a preacher, Sheikh Kitmitto, which I found online, to point me in the right direction: 'What does *The Hunchback of Notre-Dame* talk about? It talks about a poor, miserable man, who is suffering … But this man is a Jew. He used deformity to extort people.'

Victor Hugo's hunchback was a Jew! Learning that, the pieces came together. That rainy night in Melbourne, when I pulled up in my car, the person I picked up was myself!

Fired up by this thought, I stand up on the roof.

I am the hunchback!

If I'm careful I can step a little back and forth, one foot on either side of the roof's ridge. Gaining confidence in my footing, I shuffle along.

The man in the doorway of the Black Hebrew Israelites centre wants to erase me as a Jew? Try it. You erase me, there's still the hunchback. And I am the hunchback.

I look up at the moon. My mind reels further and I remember my second date with Antoinette. We went to see *Joseph and the Amazing Technicolor Dreamcoat* at the Regent Theatre in Melbourne. Cast as the Pharaoh, former AFL footballer Shane Crawford.

Oh, what a surprise, this had the snakes slithering out of their crawlspace! They did not agree with this casting decision. Crawford is white, and this was not a story for white Australia to tell. Depending on the snake making the case, this was a story that belongs to Egyptians, people of colour or Muslims. Complaints were made known to the Regent Theatre and the Media Entertainment and Arts Alliance.

Some of the worst cultural appropriation you'll see

So many white people in turbans, head scarves, Egyptian cultural dress

They have even added a questionable dance break that sees mostly white dancers dressed in hijabs can-can their way to liberation

One of the few tokenised POC being WHIPPED (that's right they did that) on stage

Cultural consultants are not a waste of time or money

But *Joseph and the Amazing Technicolor Dreamcoat* is based on a Torah story. And I caught the Melbourne production. Those hijabs were, in fact, Jewish headscarves. The actors wearing the headscarves were playing the roles of Jews, can-canning their way to liberation. The actors taking a whipping as slaves were, too, playing the roles of Jews, enslaved in Ancient Egypt.

THE HUNCHBACK ON THE ROOF

Tear up the orchestra pits! Bring in the cultural advisers! Egyptian ones! Black ones! I'll need to pull on my sunglasses, and another pair over that, the gaslight is so blinding. People are holding a 'conversation on cultural erasure' about a musical based on a Torah story and no one mentions the Jews. Trying to erase me as surely as the Black Hebrew Israelite tried.

I continue along the roof.

Silence, gentile snakes! I will make a ruling on whether footballer Shane Crawford can play the Pharaoh in the story of my people: my decision is yes.

I pause on the rooftop. I look to my numb feet and gently sit back down, pulling my knees to my chest.

Feel free to do Quasimodo too, Shane.

THE BLACK HOLE

Perched on this roof, I'm so cold that the abrasions on my skin from climbing up here don't even register as pain. The darkness, the slope, the precariousness ... I really just want to stay put. But sitting here like Buddha until there's daylight and I can move about with surer footing doesn't sound promising either.

I think. I've walked along the rear of the mansion so many times, the image of a maintenance ladder, affixed to a wall, is in my memory. Very faintly, but it's there.

I crawl down the rear slope of the roof, diagonally, in the direction of where I remember the ladder. On my way, I come across a white square of plastic stretched over a skylight hole, duct taped in place. I'm guessing I'm above the foam-padded recording studio.

I keep crawling along. When I arrive at the gutter, I discover my faint memory has screwed me over. There is no ladder.

I take this in. With a groan I fear has woken the neighbours,

THE BLACK HOLE

I commit. I'll climb back up to the hole in the attic, poke my head in and see if the bird will let me pass. Birds have to sleep.

Miserably, I begin my crawl. Memories of the bird's cry, more demon than bird, are tormenting me. The thought of its pink fleshy face almost has me dry-heaving again.

Then I pass by the white square of plastic stretched over the skylight hole. My frown twists into a smile.

I start picking at the duct tape that holds the plastic down. My nails bitten to the quick, my fingers numb, I can't catch the edges of the tape. I put my elbows to work, and the plastic covering the skylight starts giving. I move from my elbows to my feet. Ten good stomps from my feet and the plastic tears. I giggle.

I rip the square open the rest of the way. Blessed be God, it is the recording studio. I can only faintly make out the room, but I remember it: once I'm dangling from the lip of the skylight, I'll have to fall the distance of roughly one John Safran, but it'll be onto beautiful soft foam.

I reach into the round hole and feel about. The foam that pads the ceiling is thick. Lowering my entire arm down, only my fingers reach past the foam.

I cup my hands together and blow into them, to alleviate the numbing cold. I grip the outer lip of the skylight and thread myself into the dark hole.

Now inside, holding on tight, I'm yet to unbend my arms or lower my legs. I'm balled up, snuggled in by the ceiling foam.

I slowly unball until I'm dangling, my body stretched out, my arms shaking. Peeking around, I wonder if the foam that lines the floor is as thick as the foam lining the ceiling. I look down.

My memory was wrong. There is no foam lining the floor. I'll be hitting hard wood.

And the fall is more than one John Safran. It's more like a John Safran and a half.

My mind, independent of me, has done the calculations: I won't be able to hold on for much longer. This is yet another point of no return. I decide to delay my execution until my grip gives out.

In all this, a new notion hits.

I was just on a roof. I was Fiddler on the Roof! How did I miss that? It's just so *obvious*. I want to kick myself. And if I'm going to kick myself, I better do it now, because I fear both my legs will break once my grip fails and I plummet down.

In that musical, if I recall correctly – or at least it's something like this – the symbolism of the fiddler on the roof is as follows. For the man to retain his Jewishness, his traditions, as the world around him rolls forward, is a precarious game – like balancing on a roof. It's just too tempting to relax, to give it up, to assimilate. A Jew must ruminate over his place in the world.

So, I'm not the hunchback. I'm the Fiddler on the Roof. Or at least, the Fiddler Dangling from the Roof.

DANGLE

Let me think this through as I dangle. There is another reading of what's going on in that musical. Because really it's the non-Jews in the Russian village who make the fiddler's footing precarious. The Jews are conditionally accepted, but that can change on a whim. And it does. At the end of the musical the Jews are driven out of the village by order of the Tzar.

Please don't call me paranoid. The Jew is an archetypal character in the worldview of Christianity (killed Christ), Islam (descendants of apes and pigs), the far-right (puppetmasters), the far-left (the ultimate colonisers, Zionists). You can't tell me none of that can catch fire in dangerous ways. And as the years have rolled on, it's only become knottier and more contorted.

Case in point, the man of the hour. Kanye is a Black white-supremacist far-right Christian who thinks he is the real Jew. And he has millions of fans! I mean, I dig his tunes, I like his lols and trolls, but he is still painting the Jews as maniacal. Some of his fans are going to take that and run with it.

It's Kanye, the Tzar and the snakes who need to be dangling here, reckoning with the place of Jews in the world, not me.

THE FALL

I fall.

Squirming on my side, I'm rubbing my palms over my calves and ankles, in something approximating a massage. But I can still wriggle and stretch everything that needs to be wriggled and stretched.

So my prediction is that, in a few hours, I'll be able to kick myself.

I lie on my side for I don't know how long. The stars I can see through the skylight move over time.

I fall asleep.

NEXT MORNING: DAY SEVEN

I Quasimodo-hobble out of the padded room, down the blue hallway and towards the white wormhole. I thought my legs would have recovered by now, but it feels like I've sprained my ankle. I push on down the wormhole, out of the mansion, into the front grounds.

I limp, limp, limp along, past the SHERP, and stagger towards the two-storey house. I turn the golden doorknob and open to the room of Holocaust monkeys, minus the one I dragged to the SHERP. As I make my way to the staircase, I'm picturing David Cole, the Holocaust Revisionist with whom I drank Bellinis, counting the monkeys in this room. *The official figures just don't add up! We are one monkey short!*

Figuring out my body, I find that climbing the staircase with stiffened legs, step by step by step, is the least painful approach. I curve around the corner of the staircase, the halfway point. The agony is not subsiding, it's going the other way – I hadn't felt it in my knees until now.

DAY SEVEN

Kanye's bedroom is as I left it. A packet of jerky on the bedside table, a bloodied sheet balled up on the floor. I hold on to the edge of the mattress and lower myself to my knees. I scramble through the mess on the floor. Where is it?

I frantically throw items about. This makes no sense. It's gone.

I lower my head to the ground. I breathe a sigh of relief – it's under the bed. I reach my arm under and retrieve it. *Field Guide to Birds of California.*

I open to the table of contents. I don't know what to look for. My finger runs down the list. Buzzard? Eagle? Turkey?

I'm stopped in my tracks. Turkey vulture. I turn to the page and shiver. There it is, staring at me. That's what the ornithologists anointed it. Turkey vulture.

I tear the page from the book and fold it in my pocket. This was not a figment of my imagination. And anyone who tells me otherwise, I will pull the page from my pocket and flap it before them.

HEART PILLS

I squat before the gate. I retrieve the latest Egg McMuffin and a brown paper bag filled with my boxes of pills.

The agony is not just in my legs or my scraped skin – I'm feeling a sickness in my belly. And that feels connected to the throbbing in my head. I am grasping for an explanation for this pain. Maybe I shouldn't have drunk all that rainwater? But rainwater's safe. It's the *original* water. How can it not be safe? But what in God's name do I know. The scientists put fluoride in the water. If rainwater is so safe, why do the scientists put in the fluoride?

Maybe rainwater is safe except if there are chemtrails.

I need water for my pills and Kanye won't pay his bills so the taps don't work. But – yes, yes, yes there's a stream. Fresh running water. And right beneath this bridge on which I squat. I can hear it flowing, right now, beneath the concrete.

UNDER THE BRIDGE

I am safe here, sitting on the muddy bank under the bridge. No one can see through concrete.

I pull out six boxes from the brown paper bag and spread them on the bank. It's six boxes, not seven, because one of the pills I take twice a day.

I break a pill from a silver blister pack and rest it on my tongue. I cup my hands and bring water from the stream to my mouth. I gulp.

How did I suffer miniature heart attacks and not take myself to a doctor? If I was out walking, I'd brush it off as back-related or COVID-related. I'd sit down at a tram stop bench, or whatever was around, then order an Uber to take me home, where I'd fall asleep and wake up fresh.

I break out another and cup the fresh stream water into my mouth.

One evening, walking home from a friend's place, I felt the by now familiar tightness in my chest. But I was so close to home, I felt it would be too socially awkward to order an Uber to take me such a short distance. I leant against the wall of a building for what must have been half an hour, then hobbled home, having to stop five or six times, for ten minutes or so, to recover.

I swallow my third pill.

The next morning, the doctor sat across from me in his office slack-jawed, asking why I hadn't called for an ambulance the night before. Or on any of the other occasions over the past couple of months when my chest had tightened. I explained my working theory, that the pain in my chest was connected to the pain in my back, the result of jogging in sneakers that lacked sufficient support, so all could be fixed with a trip to Foot Locker. He told me I needed to visit a cardiologist, and I needed to do it that day.

I look up the stream to where I crossed the log a week ago. My eyesight can't quite make the distance. As an alternative to the Egg McMuffin wrapper, when Antoinette had something to communicate, she could have floated her message down in a bottle.

Another pill.

The cardiologist asked about my lifestyle. Alcohol? Exercise? Diet? Then he came to: Smoking?

I said, 'Funny you should ask.'

I hadn't smoked my entire life, but I had started eighteen months before the first tightening in my chest. Philip Morris International, the tobacco giant, were releasing a new cigarette that they claimed was a healthier alternative to regular cigarettes. Getting wind that this was a dodgy claim, I headed out to investigate, to debunk them. But, for my writing, I needed to lose myself in it all, so for eighteen months I chain-smoked both their regular cigarettes and their supposed healthier alternative.

The cardiologist concluded, 'Yep, that would do it.'

By the end of that week, I was laid out on an operating table, and he slid a stent into my artery. I have a stent in my heart for art.

I hope this story goes some way to explain: this house is freaking me out, it's bad for my health, but I'm finishing this.

I take my last two pills.

A DUCK DRIFTS BY

I don't feel like returning to the mansion yet. I lie down on the muddy bank under the bridge, exhausted. From either side, tall and fat cypress trees make their presence known. Looming.

I close my eyes. I wonder what all those people are up to this very moment. Professor Griff, Moonface, Elvis Costello, my fellow Melbournian Bianca Censori.

A couple of months before I left Australia for Los Angeles, I wanted to find out if the word Censori meant something, like Safran meant either red locks or saffron crocus farmers. And, looking into her family tree, one thing led to another. Could what I read be true? Or was this some other Censori? If you read a Smith had been caught riding an elephant through the park, you're not going to assume it's your colleague, Greg Smith.

So I drove to Melbourne's West, to a warehouse in a semi-industrial area. Through the windows I made out air-hockey tables, pinball machines and claw games; this business supplied these wares.

A DUCK DRIFTS BY

A bell tinkled as I pushed through the glass door. Yes, Bianca's father was the Censori who ran the place. He was friendly but bewildered that, after so many years, a writer had walked in to ask about *that*. He said he understood why I was interested, he liked reading stories of families himself, but politely ushered me out.

This man's brother, Bianca Censori's uncle, was one of the last men sentenced to death in Australia, in 1982. The uncle had murdered a waiter. I had no idea Western Australia still sentenced people to death then. Ultimately the government commuted his death sentence to life in prison, and he was freed on parole twelve years later.

I started calling landline after landline, Censori after Censori in the phonebook. So many disconnected lines. But this made me want him more. He was alive, but where? I looked at booking flights to a small town in Queensland, where chances were he wasn't living, but it was the only lead I had. This plan was only abandoned because I needed to come here.

A ROCK

This stream has helped me wash down my seven pills, but I realise it can do much more. I'm covered in a film of grime. I'll start with my face.

On my hands and knees, at the bottom of the bank, I peer into the stream. Why have I been wiping myself down with squares of baby wipes from the camping shop all week? God has granted me the gift of fresh running water and I have been dabbing myself with wipes, siphoning rainwater from a tub into empty sake bottles and boiling elbows in water from the bucket accepting a drip.

I thrust my head into the beautiful fresh water.

Pain jolts through my body. I pull back. I'm writhing in the mud, cradling my forehead with both hands.

A rock. I hit my head on a rock. I paid God a compliment and He backstabs me in the face.

MEANING

I can't see blood on my hands, but I can feel a lump on my forehead. I don't know if that was God or the house or neither of them, but this will not stop me. Yes, I'm hurting. And, thanks to this writhing, dirtier than before I went to clean myself. But the pain has shot to every nerve in my body; every nerve is feeling something, something intense; this is not only the moment to keep writing, it's the moment to find the meaning in it all. The meaning of the last week living in Kanye's mansion, and in Kanye's head. Mentally bumbling, like a monk sealed inside a monastery. The SHERP, the slave ships, the Saffron, the Holocaust, all of it!

Okay, how about this? I've been stewing over this since 1997. My appearance on *Race Around the World*. Eight young Australians, who had never been on television before, travelling to different destinations filming short documentaries. Except that, according to one judge, I wasn't a real Australian. Not like my rival, a true Aussie battler. I was filed under 'inner city bohemian who doesn't understand real Australians'. Battler? In a John Safran exclusive, let me reveal that my 'battler' rival's parents were oil magnates.

After my week in Kanye's mansion, I have realised the distinction between my rival and me was that his accent bounced along like a lovable larrikin's, while I squeaked like a Jew.

Safran, this is good. This is it.

I rise from the muddy bank, hands cupping the lump on my forehead.

I am pointing a finger at you, white Australia, and I am condemning you.

Matt Stone said it in his kitchen: 'You could pick you and me out of a line-up. You could line us up with a bunch of people and they'd probably go, *you and you.* I don't know what that is.'

What a great ending to my book. You white Australians will not let me be one of you. I am Paul Hogan. I am Hoges. Maaaaate, I confronted a turkey vulture like Hoges did with the water buffalo in *Crocodile Dundee*. But I am the *you* in a line-up. Because I'm Jewish, I can never be Australian.

I fall to my knees on the muddy bank. Now that I've got it out of my system, I realise I didn't land the plane. What in hell's name was that about? I disavow it all.

I need to calm down, I need to calm down.

I'm out of here tomorrow morning, the plan laid out on an Egg McMuffin wrapper by Antoinette. I'll wake up at 5 am. That'll give me an hour to thread back through the woods whence I came one week ago. Once I make my way through that, I'll cross back over the stream. I'll climb down the bank, walk over the log. Once safely across, I'll climb the bank on the other side and slip through the gap between the fence and the bushes. Antoinette will be waiting on the street. We'll make our getaway in the Jeep.

It'll be a relief to sleep legally for the first time in a week. This is out of my system. You can only break into three properties for art. That's the rule, I've decided. Three strikes and you're out. I breached Kanye's schoolhouse in the woods of Simi Valley, the Drakeless estate in Hidden Hills, and this mansion in the woods of Calabasas.

In my head, I play back that day in Hidden Hills. Antoinette had let me know her feelings about that break-in. *You keep putting yourself at risk by trespassing into properties. You say you're just knocking on a door.* And she brought up something else I hadn't considered until now. *You're trespassing in someone's home with security cameras everywhere.*

I lie back down on the muddy bank, still holding my lump, which is becoming a bump, which is becoming an egg.

Yes, there would have been security cameras at Château Drakeless. But the worst thought I've had in my entire life hits me harder than the rock. From lying flat in the mud, I spring into a sitting position. How are there not cameras everywhere on this property? How is there not a camera on me now?

CAMERAS

Splashing through the big blue room in the mansion, I scope every corner of the ceiling. I can't see anything, but there must be something. It is outside the scope of reality that a celebrity builds a mansion in Calabasas and doesn't install cameras. Non-celebrities have cameras linked to their phones; Antoinette has been checking on her rabbits in Sydney from LA.

Squishing toadstools underfoot, I'm slowly making my way around the room, scrutinising little holes that could house cameras. This is needle-in-a-haystack stuff.

I decide to check around the property for obvious security cameras, the kind that I imagine in my head: black glass eyes with red flashing dots.

I hobble up the wormhole, turn into the blue hallway, and begin checking the blue rooms on either side. Why can't I see any cameras?

I limp out to the front grounds. How long was I out on that

CAMERAS

muddy bank? Why is it dusk now? I begin hobbling my way to the two-storey house.

I'm thinking about Mosab Hassan Yousef, the son of one of the founders of Hamas. He defected to Israel in 1997 and went on to spy for Israel.

I finally make it past the SHERP and the garage, albeit much slower than before I fell through the hole.

The United Israel Appeal brought Mosab to Melbourne to tell his story. Of course, I went along.

I reach the golden doorknob of Kanye's two-storey house.

Mosab was speaking at a big white mansion, one suburb up from mine. Walking in from the street, I was confounded. There were no armed guards, no unarmed guards, no metal detectors, not even a list where they checked off your name.

I stagger around Kanye's bedroom. I can't find any cameras.

Hundreds of guests sat around their tables, listening to Mosab's story. As I looked around, I thought there was zero chance a Zionist group had organised a speaking tour for a defector from Hamas – the son of one of the founders! – and was, like, *Hey, now that you mention it, John, there is no security. It didn't occur to us.* No, there was another option. There was some next-level security system – whatever it was – so sophisticated, you're not even going to see it. The Israeli secret service has it. Billionaires have it. Kanye has it.

Back outside, I look up. The scaffolding. I bet the cameras are in the scaffolding. Clipped to the top of the poles, looking down. The cops have cameras on poles at the 7-Eleven car park in your street, John. Why wouldn't Kanye have them?

I'm on a hard drive. Seven days on a hard drive.

My legs don't hurt anymore, because there's something more important. I move up the side of the two-storey house and circle to the back of the property. I trip because I'm eyeing the top of the poles rather than looking where I'm going.

I skirt past the rear of the two-storey house. My eyes fall from the poles to the white cottage. That weird house. Locked door. Everything else here is unlocked. And a mail slot in the door and a door mat. When the rest of this place is falling apart. Toadstools and skylights collapsing. Here's a tidy and neat doorway, like this cottage sits in a normal street in a nice normal suburb. This is where the CCTV recordings are being kept.

I throw myself against the door.

Backing up, preparing myself for my second throw, I see the mudprint left by my ear when I pressed it against the door at the start of the week.

I throw myself again.

I am the madman who does the same thing again and again and expects a different result.

I'm on the hard drive. I will get in.

I bet it's more high-tech than the image in my head, but there's a bank of monitors behind that door. These days, no doubt there's audio too. You go around with your bleeding-edge audio recorder, John. I think we can safely say billionaires' CCTV systems are taping sound, too.

There will be a way in through the roof of the cottage. There are skylights everywhere else. There were scores of tools lining the wall in the garage, there must be a ladder in there too.

RETURNING TO THE COTTAGE

Everything in me – every cell, the stent in my heart, every bead of sweat rolling down my face – is coming together so I can focus on the locked white door of the cottage.

I roll my shoulders, I lift the axe, I bring it down. Splinters fly. I yank it from the wood, I bring it down, splinters fly.

The wood yields. The axe has torn a long, narrow hole.

Five more strikes and there is space enough to thread my arm in.

I navigate my hand through the splintered wood and reach around until I find the deadlock. It surrenders a click.

I creak open the damaged door. The hinges are askew but only offer a little resistance.

I'm squinting, begging my eyes to hurry up and adjust to the darkness.

What is this? Even in the dim light I can make out a shock of colour everywhere. The same colour.

My fingers find a light switch by the doorway and flick.

There is no bank of monitors.

I stagger in. I'm standing in the middle of a room surrounded by what must be thousands of books, stacked floor to ceiling. And it's all the one book. Repetition after repetition of the same orange spine.

I approach one of these towers and gingerly wiggle out a copy. I hold it up and read the cover: *Raising Kanye: Life lessons from the mother of a hip-hop superstar,* by Donda West with Karen Hunter.

I limp into another room. Cardboard boxes are stacked about in here. I approach one box, unpick the duct tape and unfold the flaps. More copies of *Raising Kanye*.

I've come across so many strange things in this mansion this week – things I haven't understood – but I immediately know what's going on here. My family has done the same thing for me, albeit at a more modest scale.

Kanye's mother released a book and he wanted to support her, so he bought some copies. Thousands of copies. Kanye's a good guy.

I poke around to get my bearings. This place was not built to warehouse books; it was built for a live-in groundskeeper or someone like that. The room stacked with cardboard boxes also contains a single bed, pushed against a wall, along with a small bedside table. The bed is made up, and it wouldn't look out of place in an army barracks or motel, so neat and squared off are the sheets and blanket. A box sits upon it. A spongy couch is pushed against another wall, which I suspect was moved from the front room to make space for the towers of books.

RETURNING TO THE COTTAGE

I open a cupboard and find a few piles of neatly folded linen, and another door slides open to a small en suite bathroom. I'm startled by my reflection in the mirror, the purple egg on my head from hitting it on the rock. This is the first mirror I've discovered besides the little one in the SHERP.

I leave the bedroom. I pass through the front room and to the room on the other side, which is a kitchenette. All the essentials: a stove, a sink, a pantry and a coffee percolator. A chair is tucked under the counter, which must serve as a table. The bar fridge is humming. I open it to six bottles of water, plastic-wrapped together. The pantry holds salt, pepper and other condiments, a jar of coffee and not much else.

The overhead lights are working, so I'm not surprised the red light comes on when I plug in the coffee percolator. I fill the percolator with bottled water from the fridge, tip the coffee into the filter, and leave it to brew.

Back in the bedroom, I remove the cardboard box from the bed. This leaves a bright diamond shape in the dust covering the white cotton blanket.

I don't want to deal with the dust when I sleep here tonight. I peel off the cotton blanket, throw it in the cupboard and take a fresh blanket from the pile of linen.

Everything feels in order now. I've pushed a cardboard box against the damaged door to ensure it remains shut and poured myself a cup of coffee. Now I'm propped up in the bed. All the lights in the cottage are switched off except for the lamp on the bedside table. I begin reading *Raising Kanye: Life lessons from the mother of a hip-hop superstar* by Donda West.

It soon becomes apparent Kanye's mother, like my mother, is a far better person than her son.

Donda was mindful when it came to the feelings of others. She loved a man, but could see young Kanye was unhappy around him, so she ended the relationship. But she made sure she didn't break the man's heart. She tried to teach Kanye balance – that you can follow your creative impulses, that it's a wonderful thing, but you shouldn't be disrespectful to others.

And I learn Kanye owed it to her, filling this cottage with her book. The day of the release of his first album, *College Dropout*, she walked into a record shop and bought ten copies. The next week she returned and did it again. My mum bought multiple copies of my 1997 novelty single 'Not The Sunscreen Song', although she hit different record shops, to throw the Australian Recording Industry Association off the scent. My mother died age fifty-eight of a heart attack, as Donda had.

Our mothers held other things in common. Kanye, who airs his grievances about colleagues, family and strangers, can't find a bad word to say about his mother. Same. Even digging deep to retrieve a story about my mother that casts her in a bad light, this is all I have: as a kid, our family computer was set up on a desk outside my bedroom door, and late at night I'd hear the sound of her clicking and dragging the mouse, playing Solitaire. That's it.

For whatever reason, when I found out my mother had died, I didn't cry. Not at her funeral, either. But months later, veteran Australian actress Jacki Weaver came up to me in a foyer outside a film-awards ceremony. I knew of her, of course, but we had never met. She said, 'I wish you were my son.' After we finished talking,

RETURNING TO THE COTTAGE

I headed to the bathroom, closed the cubicle door behind me and started crying, the sound of cocaine being cut and snorted coming from the cubicles on either side.

MOTHER COMES TO PICK ME UP

Antoinette pulls up outside Kanye's mansion. Her cheerful face contorts when she catches the purple lump on my forehead. She looks like she might cry. She asks if I'm okay. I tell her I am. I can tell she doesn't believe me.

She's finding it hard to maintain eye contact, distracted by the purple egg. She asks why I've emptied out the duffle bags on the road. I tell her I've realised I left my pills inside the mansion. And why aren't I wearing shoes? I tell her I left my only pair of socks in the oven too long and they were destroyed.

She points to the pair of shoes lying on the road among my belongings and asks what's wrong with those. I wrinkle my forehead, thinking it through. I destroyed my socks ... but why did I forget I could still wear my shoes without them?

Finally accepting my pleas that the egg on my forehead looks worse than it feels, but insisting we head to the nearest pharmacy, cheer returns to Antoinette's face. I learn there are things that wouldn't fit on Egg McMuffin wrappers. While I've been inside the mansion, she's been on her own adventure, helping Rabbit Sanctuary, who rescue and rehome rabbits back in Australia. Before we left for America, Antoinette rescued one such rabbit from a pet store.

'Tony was in a glass fish tank – a repurposed fish tank. He couldn't really hop back and forth.'

She encouraged people to leave critical Google reviews about the store, part of a chain owned by Woolworths. One thing led to another, and this week the supermarket giant stopped selling pets.

'One rabbit shut down thirty-three pet stores. You can thank Tony for that. Just being a rabbit, just existing, surviving through it all.'

THE CASTING CALL

In a diner, laptop open, I'm punching away madly on the airline's ticket site, trying to figure out how to delay my flight back to Australia. An opportunity has arisen, posted on Donda's Place, a Kanye-affiliated Instagram account: *yzy casting beings with shaved heads 3 – 6pm 923 E 3rd St Los Angeles, CA 90013.*

Yeezy needs models. For what, I'm not exactly sure. But the open casting is today.

'Do you reckon they mean clean shaven or just short?'

'You've got to shave your head,' Antoinette says, giggling at the madness of it all. 'All your little golden locks.'

The taxi driver lets me out at the only barbershop I can find open on a Sunday, in Harvard Heights, Central Los Angeles. Making my way in, the barber is speaking Spanish to the man planted in the barber's chair. I settle in the waiting area. One wall is lined with paintings of heads, showcasing different hairstyles. Out of the dozens of haircut recommendations, none is a bald head.

I'm soon invited to the barber's chair.

'Zero,' I say as the barber wraps the tissue around my neck.

'Seguro?' By his raised eyebrows I gauge this means something like 'You sure?'

'Zero.'

He barely suppresses a wince. The clipper starts to shear, the golden locks tumble to the floor.

Bzzzzzzzzzzzzzzz.

Exiting the barbershop, returning to the same taxi, I feel the breeze on my scalp.

'You look handsome now,' the driver says. 'Better than before.'

He is bald himself, so let's factor that into his review.

I clock myself in the rear-view mirror. My head is a nice shape, I gotta say.

When we arrive in the Arts District in downtown LA, several hundred other hopefuls are already lining up. The casting call didn't specify what to wear, but everyone knew to turn up in black. All heads are various degrees of bald.

As I join the line, I spot the bouncer filing people inside in batches. It's Moonface! I fear he'll be furious when he spots me. But in a delicious twist of fate, now that I'm a moonface too, he doesn't recognise me. I swan by unnoticed.

Inside, the reception area is generic and modern – a front desk, a couch, doors leading to other rooms. But one item stands out: an imposing wooden chair with a Christian cross carved into it. Instead of an archbishop, upon the chair sits a stack of papers. A hypebeast holding a clipboard wanders around, handing out legal agreements. With a smile, she says we must sign them, then place them on the wooden chair. We're told to leave our phones in a tub, then we're ushered up a staircase in groups of three.

Upstairs, two female contenders and I are directed to one side. Across the room, a panel of judges sits behind a table. Kanye isn't one. Nor is Bianca Censori. But they all look like Bianca. Who, in turn, looks like Kim Kardashian.

A hypebeast approaches, asking us to remove our shoes, which we do. He then explains that the female contenders should leave their tops on, but the males must remove theirs.

My black t-shirt comes off smoothly, over my zero-cut bald head. I'm usually up for anything, although this instruction catches me off-guard, so I'm not feeling entirely comfortable. As we make our way across the room, I ponder whether my body is in as good a shape as my head. We catwalk towards the Biancas, around and behind their table, then catwalk back again. With a smile, one asks for a second saunter, and after that, a third.

'Thank you,' one of the Biancas says. She informs us that successful candidates will get a call back.

A CLOSE SHAVE

I did not get a call back.

So the next night, I'm standing outside the event I had auditioned for, in a line of Kanye fanatics. We're outside a warehouse in the Melrose Avenue district. It's near midnight. The diehards have come out: they know in their hearts that Kanye won't be here, but they are willing to chance it.

Melrose Avenue hosts a fair share of clothing stores – including an Adidas one. After being fired, Kanye felt compelled to respond; basically a John Safran with more money, driven by pettiness, he decided to lease the shop next door to Adidas. No one was sure how he'd make use of it in the long term, and no one is entirely sure how he'll be using it tonight.

We are gathered on a leafy residential street outside the actual shopping precinct, by a warehouse space at the back of the store. The queue is bustling. A woman strolls by who, to me, is Kim Kardashian. But she can't be her, because no one is turning their head.

Landing in Los Angeles from Sydney, I couldn't tell the difference: Kmart shopper or hypebeast? But now my eye has developed. Well, isn't that a nice Bathing Ape jacket you're sporting, my friend.

I am soon threading into the back entrance of the warehouse along with everyone else. Outside, streetlights fought the night. Inside, stout white candles line the walls of this dark space. Whatever is going to happen isn't happening yet. The rectangular room is split in two, with men dressed in black, holding small torches, telling us to stick to our half. No barricade prevents us from disobeying this order – it is a gentlemen's agreement.

This isn't an expansive space. There is room for scores, not hundreds. The walls and low ceiling are unpainted wood. I have lost my bearings and sense of space: are these walls cordoning us off from a much bigger area we'll be moving into or is this it? I glance up to what looked to be a skylight, letting in the blue sky. Then I remember it's midnight, the painted square playing tricks on my eyes.

Frank Ocean's 'Self Control' plays, and then, without a breath, plays again, then again, washing over me. Dreamy, ethereal synths, soft percussion and lush vocals. Played once, it was 'the song'; on loop it becomes disorienting and hypnotic.

Finally, models emerge from a cavity in the wall. Flamelight from the hundreds of candles light up these young men and women from below. They step slowly, in unison, single file, staring ahead glumly. They assemble in rows before us. I can count two dozen. All fitted in black pants and tight t-shirts that reveal no one has a beer gut. It is impossible to tell in this light if the t-shirts are white or cream.

Their gaunt, miserable faces match the most attention-grabbing feature on these models: every head is shaved. I scratch my naked scalp. These are the candidates who beat me out. By a slim margin, most of the models are white, with Asians, Blacks and Latinos peppered in. It is as if Auschwitz had been more diverse.

The rows of models stare through us, the Frank Ocean song looping, the crowd mesmerised, silent, swaying. Feeling the sting of rejection I begin thinking, one sharp kick of the candles and this place might go up.

Half an hour later the models turn and file out, returning to the cavity whence they came. Now the security men, waving their small torches towards the exit, begin shepherding the crowd out. An organiser steps out of the cavity. She is unhappy, feeling some of the crowd are dragging their feet.

'Let's go,' the organiser instructs. 'You cannot stay here, you cannot stay here.'

Adding to her stress, several models have exited the cavity to mingle with their friends in the crowd.

'If you're a model and you have a white t-shirt, stay here.'

Some of the crowd are pleading their case, but she is not swayed. I'm not judging anyone – I want to stay and see what happens next too.

Dawdling around the room, I spot a walkie-talkie resting on the ground and, beside it, a small torch. I lean down and scoop up the torch. I start wandering about, ushering people out, along with the other men bearing torches. Soon the room is clear of those who do not belong, the music turns down, the lights turn on, and the rest of the models come back out.

The organiser asks the models to huddle up, she has something she wants to tell them.

'Thank you so much,' she begins. 'Every single one of you. You are all part of the family, the army, and we're going to be working on other shows soon. So we'll be in touch with all of you guys. And I just wanted to say thank you. You can keep your shirts too.'

One of the female models pipes up. 'Are we getting paid?'

The organiser appears unprepared for this question.

'Are you getting paid?' she says, repeating the question to give her time to formulate a response. 'Maybe for the next show.'

'So, no?' the model says, wanting clarification.

'So, yeah, no. This was more of a shirt thing.'

The model wants details about this next show, the one where payment is being promised (maybe). Is every model who took part tonight going to be offered a spot?

'I can't discuss all the details now because I don't have them. I just want to say thank you.'

I feel the applause that follows is lighter than it would have been had the model not spoken up.

The organiser says anyone who doesn't have a car and needs a ride should see her. Ten or so models take her up on this offer. If they are expecting cab vouchers, they are not in luck. The organiser can't offer anyone transport directly home, but says she can get them downtown if that is of help. A few models take her up on this. The organiser now whistles to grab the attention of all the models in the room. She asks if anyone has a car and can give these guys a lift downtown.

A CLOSE SHAVE

Exiting the warehouse, the fresh air hitting my face, I think of Kanye and pull my audio recorder to my lips.

'Can you believe that motherfucker is blaming the Jews for exploiting artists?'

THE KIDS

The crowd mills around on the street, not ready to leave just yet. Every conversation soon falls into excited speculation over where Kanye might turn up.

I catch a Star of David dangling from the neck of a young guy chatting with a couple of his friends and wander over. He asks what I'm doing in LA. I tell them I've been squatting at Kanye's Calabasas mansion. His eyes light up.

'Went *inside*?' He can't believe it.

'How'd you get in?' his friend gasps.

I tell them about the fence that must be slipped through, the stream that must be forded, the woods that must be hiked. I pull out the Yemulke from my bag and the three of them practically faint.

They might be diehard enough to turn up tonight, but they're still torn about the man of the hour.

The kid with the necklace says, 'So tonight: all bald, all in uniform. What do you think he was trying to mock?'

'I know what you're about to say,' I reply. 'Whether he did it subconsciously or —'

'No, it was on purpose. You shave a bunch of people's heads and you put them in uniform. What else can you mean? You know?'

I take this in. Kanye went defcon on the Jews, but I struck back and commandeered his mansion. I thought I'd won, come out on top. But that's not true. He's sending me home with a shaved head.

JONAH AND THE WHALE

Four hours before our flight back to Australia, Antoinette and I are slumped across the seats at the gate at LAX, killing time.

'You were like Jonah in the whale,' Antoinette says.

In that Torah story, God tells Jonah he needs to warn the people of an impending disaster. Jonah doesn't think he's up for the task, so he tries to flee God, jumping on a boat. But rough seas sent by God threaten to upturn the boat, and when the crew finds out it's Jonah who God is after, they toss him into the ocean. There, Jonah is swallowed by a whale. For three days and three nights, he is cut off from the world, forced into a state of introspection, ruminating over his life – what he has learnt and what he needs to pass on.

When the whale vomits him out onto a beach, Jonah is changed. He now knows he has to confront certain truths, no matter how uncomfortable.

The mansion, too, has vomited me out changed.

People, I have come here with a warning. We never know when things are going to catch fire. Who would have thought a Black American celebrity would be the one to introduce old, esoteric European conspiracies to a new generation.

Antisemites warn the world that Jews are tricky with words, but what I've realised is that *they* are the ones who've weaponised a word. 'Conspiracy' is just a nasty way of saying 'community' and 'solidarity'. They're trying to make us loosen our grip on what has saved us over millennia. We're a small community – 0.2 per cent of the world's population – and yet people who don't like us pathologise it when we stick together. But sticking together is what helped my grandparents rebuild their lives when they came to Australia after the Holocaust. When my grandfather, a cobbler, resoled Mr Goldberg's loafers, he only charged for materials, not labour. And when Mr Goldberg built a cabinet for my grandparents, he did the same. The cabal! The Jewish octopus!

So now I have emerged from the mansion to stand before you, as Jonah stood before his people, to tell you that solidarity is a good card to have in your pocket.

KANYE WAS RIGHT

When I stand up to get a coffee from the airport food court, Antoinette grabs the cap from my head. She says I need to embrace my new look because it'll be a while until my golden locks return. But at the coffee shop, the woman behind the counter won't meet my gaze. I'm learning people don't like to make eye contact when they think you're going through chemotherapy.

Once I've placed my order, she motions at the card reader. I pluck out my credit card, thinking about Kanye and how he's responsible for my shaved head. I decide to slide this credit card back into my wallet and pull out a different one. This one is silver – it looks a bit magic. I feel over the raised lettering. Kanye West.

I should be more prudent. Will this go through? If it does, can this be tracked? Is this one of those things where, if you're busted, they ring the Australian embassy?

I tap it on the card reader. Hey, Kanye, a Jew is reaching into your bank account.

BEEP.

ACKNOWLEDGEMENTS

I count myself so lucky to work with editor Johannes Jakob, publisher Nikki Christer and the team at Penguin Random House. I'm grateful for the management of Kevin Whyte, Claire Harrison and the folks at Creative Representation. Additional thanks to the rabbit community.